# Developing Teacher
# Assessment

# Developing Teacher Assessment

*John Gardner, Wynne Harlen,*
*Louise Hayward and Gordon Stobart,*
*with Martin Montgomery*

Mc Graw Hill   Open University Press

Open University Press
McGraw-Hill Education
McGraw-Hill House
Shoppenhangers Road
Maidenhead
Berkshire
England
SL6 2QL

email: enquiries@openup.co.uk
world wide web: www.openup.co.uk

and Two Penn Plaza, New York, NY 10121-2289, USA

First published 2010

A catalogue record of this book is available from the British Library

ISBN-13: 978 0 335 23783 8 (pb)   978 0 335 23782 1 (hb)
ISBN-10: 0335237835 (pb)   0335237827 (hb)

Library of Congress Cataloging-in-Publication Data
CIP data has been applied for

Fictitous names of companies, products, people, characters and/or data that
may be used herein (in case studies or in examples) are not intended to
represent any real individual, company, product or event.

Typeset by Aptara Inc., India
Printed in the UK by Bell and Bain Ltd., Glasgow

**Mixed Sources**
Product group from well-managed
forests and other controlled sources
www.fsc.org  Cert no. TT-COC-002769
© 1996 Forest Stewardship Council

*The McGraw·Hill Companies*

# Contents

*Acknowledgements*                                                    vii

**Developing teacher assessment: an introduction**                     1
*John Gardner*


## Part I: Lighting the fuse

**1   Assessment to support learning**                                15
*Wynne Harlen and John Gardner*

**2   What is quality teacher assessment?**                           29
*Wynne Harlen*

**3   What is happening in the UK?**                                  53
*Martin Montgomery*


## Part II: Spreading the word, widening the practice

**4   What is innovative about teacher assessment?**                  71
*John Gardner*

**5   Moving beyond the classroom**                                  85
*Louise Hayward*

**6   Professional learning to support teacher assessment**          100
*Wynne Harlen*

**7   Teachers as self-agents of change**                            130
*John Gardner*

# Part III: Keeping it going

**8 Making a difference: evaluating the impact of innovations in assessment** 141
*Gordon Stobart*

**9 Embedding and sustaining developments in teacher assessment** 155
*Wynne Harlen and Louise Hayward*

**Appendix 1: Projects examined and members of the core group and advisory committee of the Nuffield Foundation-funded Analysis and Review of Innovations in Assessment (ARIA) Study, 2006/8** 172

**Appendix 2: A professional development template** 174
*John Gardner*

*References* 179
*Index* 195

# Acknowledgements

In the course of our work for this book, over 200 experts from across the UK and every part of the educational community gave their time and expertise to refine our understanding of introducing change into schools across the UK. They included teachers, head teachers, researchers, local authority and government officials, inspectors, union representatives, consultants and representatives from statutory and non-statutory bodies. A smaller but still significant number of people, who were or are involved in major assessment projects, also contributed their experiences of trying to effect change through developing teacher assessment in schools. Too legion to name, we owe all of them our sincerest thanks and appreciation.

The Analysis and Review of Innovations in Assessment (ARIA) project, which has provided the empirical strength for this book, could not have proceeded so successfully without the considerable support of our Advisory Committee: Paul Black, Richard Daugherty, Kathryn Ecclestone, Mary James, Dorothy Kavanagh, Alison Kidd, Stuart Merry, Paul Newton, Catrin Roberts, Mike Walker, Anne Whipp and Martin Montgomery (who also contributed Chapter 3). A special, heartfelt 'thank you' goes to them and to both Despina Galanouli and Jo Wilson for their excellent research support.

Finally, we would very much like to thank the Nuffield Foundation for their generous support of the fieldwork and Fiona Richman of the Open University Press/McGraw-Hill for encouraging us to follow through with our ideas in the form of this book.

John Gardner, Wynne Harlen, Louise Hayward and Gordon Stobart
June 2009

# Developing teacher assessment: an introduction

*John Gardner*

## Initiative overload

For many years now, schools and colleges across the UK have been swamped by 'must do' initiatives designed to improve learning, raise standards and meet a whole host of other complex educational aspirations. The shelves of head teachers' offices overflow with glossy guidance and resource packs – some excellent, some questionable and some downright faddish. While the tally of initiative-related materials from government bodies and local authorities competes with the commercial sector's unsolicited freebies, 'initiative overload' deprives teachers of time for creativity and development. And head teachers everywhere seek shelter from what Coughlan (BBC News, 2007a) suggests is either a 10-year 'blizzard of gimmicks' or a 'golden age'. Prominent among this onslaught of innovations, however, has been the positive emergence of research-proven formative assessment or assessment for learning (AfL) as a major ally in the pursuit of improved learning and raised standards. Its benefits have been proven in many contexts since the seminal review of Black and Wiliam (1998a) and Hargreaves (2005: 9) explains its wildfire success in schools as being due to '. . . the scientific evidence and the practice evidence [being] aligned and mutually supportive'.

## Teacher assessment

Thanks to AfL, assessment by teachers has also taken on a new importance in schools and education systems around the world, as a complement or replacement for external testing. However, there remains a public concern that assessment by teachers may be untrustworthy or inconsistent between schools. There is evidence that teachers can inadvertently or otherwise undertake assessments with a degree of bias; for example, in favouring (or in some cases putting down) their own pupils.[1] And consistency between schools is an enduring challenge for any assessment system. But there is also considerable evidence that appropriate training and effective moderation processes can make teachers' judgements as sound (i.e. reliable and valid) or even more dependable than the results from any external test. And we do not need to look further than the trusted role that teachers play in many state examinations such as in first-marking their pupils' coursework for the General Certificate in Secondary Education (GCSE). Instances of plagiarism, inappropriate levels of assistance and other problems have resulted in home-based coursework being phased out, to be replaced by 'controlled' assessment approaches from 2009 onwards (QCA, 2008a). These new arrangements for coursework include fixed time periods and supervision, with the tasks defined by the examining bodies. Crucially, it was not teacher judgement that caused the change (it was more the plagiarism threats of the Internet, etc.) and teacher assessment is retained as the first-marking process followed by moderation. With some six million GCSE entries every year the teachers' role remains vital to the successful processing of this huge enterprise.

That said, GCSEs and their ilk are externally created, their marking schemes are decided without reference to the large majority of teachers and their pupils, the test-taking process is highly regulated and formal, and the bulk of their marking is carried out by examiners commissioned by an examinations body. Teacher assessment, that is assessment by teachers, is distinctly different and is experiencing a renaissance (see Chapter 3) throughout the UK. Teacher assessment is classroom-based. It is not a school-based variant of external testing where teachers design and produce tests to be taken by the school's pupils, under the auspices of the school and marked and judged by the school's staff. At present few schools would have teachers with the necessary technical skills to do this though this situation is changing as the UK Chartered Institute of Educational Assessors promotes training in all types of assessment expertise, including AfL, in UK schools. So what is distinctive about this book's approach to assessment by teachers?

The answer is enshrined in the first of 10 principles[2] we offer throughout this book, all of which are designed to guide good practice. This is the principle that *assessment of any kind should ultimately improve learning*.

As the central underpinning philosophy in good assessment practice, this is a deceptively understated principle. If our ultimate goal is to help young people to prepare and be ready for a life of learning, then arguably everything we do in education should assist that goal. Assessment processes should therefore help pupils to improve their learning as well as fulfilling other roles such as helping them to gain certification, measuring the extent of their achievements and reporting these to others. Yet it remains a distant prospect that students will receive feedback on their final university examinations, rather than simply have a line on a parchment.

Even the relatively recent development of returning GCSE scripts is primarily used to look at the quality of the marking to see if the school should appeal, rather than feed back into learning.

## Why is interest in teacher assessment growing?

There are several key influences acting to generate greater interest in assessment by teachers, not least the soaring costs of external testing, the improbability of external tests contributing effectively to learning and the potential of such testing to distort the focus of learning. This is not a new phenomenon; indeed, the potential for examinations to miss the point of 'education' was a problem alluded to by Joshua Fitch in his 1880 lectures at the University of Cambridge on teaching:

> The whole subject of examinations looms very large in the vision of the public and is apt to be seen out of its true proportions, mainly because it is the one portion of school business which is recorded in newspapers. We shall perhaps arrive at right notions about it more readily, if we first consider the business of examinations wholly subordinate to that of education, as part of the work of a school.
>
> (Fitch, 1898: 158–9)

In more recent times in the UK, external examinations have become unpopularly associated with evaluating school performance and the performance of teachers. Many support the use of external tests in high stakes situations (e.g., admission to university) but each country in the UK has at some time experienced repeated testing of pupils in both the primary and secondary sectors. This testing, though crudely claimed to provide a standards-raising challenge to pupils, has been designed primarily to enable education authorities and parents to judge how well a school is performing. One of the most invidious outcomes of such a strategy has been the ranking of schools in 'league tables' based on the pupils' performances in externally administered tests. England alone retains this use of external testing at 11 and 16 years old, despite the tests at the end of Key Stage 3 (approximately 14-year-olds) being scrapped owing to what the Schools' Secretary for England, Ed Balls, described as a marking 'shambles' (BBC News, 2008). The massed ranks of educationalists in all sectors remain vociferously opposed to the league tables though attitudes to the national curriculum assessments are more divided. There are those who oppose them on educational grounds and those who prefer them to increased use of teacher assessment, which they perceive would cause an increase in workload (BBC News, 2009).

The dominance of external testing in government policy in England has created a situation in which schools are forced continuously to improve their pupils' performance to meet externally imposed targets and standards (though clearly this could also be the case if teacher assessment was the established assessment regime). Under the worthy aspiration to raise standards, governments have wittingly or otherwise caused the indicators of their standards (e.g., national curriculum test scores for primary school reading in England) to become the objectives of the pupils' learning. One of the most damaging consequences of this is that schools may begin teaching to the tests to improve performance and meet or exceed the standards. Naturally, such a strategy must weaken attention to the wider curriculum and its learning goals. This distortion in a school's curriculum and mission must also give rise to poor motivation for pupils who do not improve sufficiently or indeed consistently fail to do well over the multiple testing occasions involved.

These problems have long been recognized by educationalists and there is significant evidence pointing to the use of assessment in support of learning as being a major and more appropriate means of assisting individual pupils to reach their potential. This does not mean that external tests should be rejected; rather, it is part of an argument that calls for the rejection of their overuse, and the educational problems to which such overuse can give rise. External testing will always be a feature of most education systems and that is how it should be. However, the complementary and currently underdeveloped role of assessment by teachers holds the promise of assessment more clearly integrated into the classroom and learning context. And this is the focus of this book – harnessing the benefits of teacher assessment in our schools.

A particularly important influence in the changes we are experiencing is the growing recognition that teachers are often best placed to provide a true picture of the learning and achievements of their pupils. In the last decade or so the huge increase in teachers' interest in AfL has in turn prompted initiatives designed to explore how classroom assessments might be used for assessment *of* learning purposes. The comprehensive understanding of a pupil's learning progress can provide appropriate performance information to replace or work in conjunction with externally set and marked tests.

At this point a good assessment 'health warning' is needed. In some important quarters there is a worrying misappropriation of the notion of classroom assessment. A key element of AfL is for teachers to adjust their teaching to take account of what they learn from these assessments, including, for example, adjusting or improving their questioning and feedback. However, the other key issues are more explicitly pupil-focused. For example, experienced teachers continuously assess where pupils are in their learning in order to help them to take charge of their own learning and to enable them to identify the next steps they should take. The teaching and learning focuses are mutually dependent, of course, but forms of didactic teaching, that is, with little or no engagement of the pupils, have not disappeared.

The health warning alarm therefore rings when the teacher – pupil interaction strays too far from a pupil-centred focus to a teacher-centred one that is a halfway house. It enables teachers to improve their teaching but may reduce the focus and explicit intention to improve learning *per se*. This is emphatically not a criticism of helping teachers to teach better but it does warn of the subtle dangers of changing focus from the pupil's learning to one in which the delivery of the teaching is the prime beneficiary. What is taught and how it is taught are still important elements in the service of better learning. The risk is that these become teacher-driven activities in which pupils play a largely passive role.

One manifestation of the potential problem would be the case in which pupils' knowledge and understanding are repeatedly assessed. For example, some 80 per cent of primary schools in England purchased 'progress' tests from the former National Assessment Agency in 2007 (BBC News, 2007b). Schools have a legitimate and worthy wish to monitor pupil progress as 'objectively' as they can, and a wide variety of commercial and state agency tests and assessment tasks is available for purchase. However, this is an unregulated and extremely varied practice that more often than not may constitute a significant overtesting of pupils across the UK.

There is also the strong potential for teacher assessment in the current Assessing Pupils' Progress arrangements for Key Stage 3 (QCA, 2009) to become merely a frequent check listing against criteria. The danger is that the pupil's control of the learning process may be lost to the gloss of beguiling phrases such as 'personalized learning' and 'diagnostic assessment'. The frequent, recorded assessments can be argued to be important feedback to individuals on their attainment, though the benefits of feedback on repeated failing might require a major stretch of the imagination. They can usefully diagnose weaknesses but if they remain a tool *only* for teachers to adjust their teaching, the process of learning may take a back seat.

Putting pupils at the centre of their own learning (clearly, no one else can do the learning for them) is a key element of AfL and the role of the teacher in this formative assessment process is a major focus of this book. So too is the role of the teacher in using the many classroom AfL interactions to draw up dependable reports (summative assessments) of a pupil's learning and achievements. The rise of such learning-oriented assessment is not restricted to the UK. It is a truly global phenomenon, charted for example in an international overview of formative assessment carried out by the Organization for Economic and Co-operative Development (OECD, 2005).

## Formative and summative

At the outset of planning this book, we recognized that the terminology of assessment may present a challenge for many teachers and for some even the distinction between *formative* and *summative* assessment may generate a distracting degree of confusion. The simple but misleading distinction is that formative assessment is what a teacher might do during a period of learning and summative assessment is what they do at the end of it. This time-based distinction is unhelpful as it ignores the purposes and contexts of the assessments, and crucially how they relate to the learning process. We will develop the distinction later but it is important at this point to lay the ghost of 'time'-related assessment opportunities.

The most important argument is that an assessment activity is not inherently formative or summative; it is the purpose and use to which it is put that determines which of these it is. If a test is used to help pupils improve their learning, then technically it is being used formatively; it is assessment *for* learing. If an assessment activity and its 'result' (e.g. a score or a comment) is used in a report of a pupil's standard of performance, then it is being used summatively; it is assessment *of* learning. Logically then, an end-of-year test can be used summatively to report performance and formatively if it is also made the focus of pupil reflection and self-evaluation of their performance. But it is worth emphasizing that the term 'formative' only applies to the use of assessments to support learning.

When asked about assessment matters, many teachers might claim not to be 'assessment literate' though in truth they may be well-versed in good formative assessment practices such as effective classroom questioning and feedback. However, they are probably more accurate in their self-assessment when it comes to techniques that are used to make an assessment of learning through such approaches as class tests. While these will undoubtedly be useful in providing teachers with one type of measure of their pupils' grasp of a topic, their technical quality in terms of test design may be more miss than hit.

But existing competence and understanding of assessment matters is not necessary to benefit from this book. Our intentions are to inform and stimulate the understanding and development of assessment practices for individuals and schools, through reading the book and through professional development activities based on the assessment issues it covers. Capturing teachers' motivation and commitment to adopting any innovation invariably requires them to be convinced of its potential to improve learning and raise standards. The process of adoption of new approaches also requires in-depth planning and commitment to ensure that any developments are undertaken in a high-quality and sustainable fashion. Subsequent chapters will therefore cover key professional learning dimensions such as the purposes of assessment, the need for evidence to support innovation, the process and steps to develop new practice, and perceptions of what counts as quality assessment in schools. Various perspectives will be considered as the book explains how teachers and schools should set about developing new practices, and how the system should react to support them.

## Key messages

The chapters in this book draw partly on our extensive experience of international and national assessment development as members of the Assessment Reform Group and partly on our UK-wide review of most of the recent initiatives in teacher assessment in the UK. This work, the ARIA study,[3] was funded by the Nuffield Foundation and combined the views of 200-plus experts, from all four countries of the UK, who came together in a series of invited seminars to discuss the key issues emerging from the various initiatives. They included teachers and head teachers, academics, inspectors of schools, education consultants, school pupils, representatives of the four teaching councils and the professional teacher associations, representatives of the curriculum and assessment bodies, and both local authority officers and government representatives.

The most important feature of the book is therefore its breadth of perspectives on the finely focused issue of teacher assessment in schools. The book's main intention is to promote the development of teacher assessment by helping the main actors in schools, local authorities and government education and teaching agencies to capitalize on the insights from both the initiatives and expert participants in ARIA, and to better appreciate the processes that drive educational innovation and change.

Among the many insights that emerged from the ARIA study, there were two main conclusions. The first was that initiatives in assessment do not always take full account of the key dimensions of the change process or the needs of the communities involved. In this sense they can often be described as being underdesigned with consequent doubts, particularly in the sustainability of any new practices. It was clear that education systems, from school to national, must fully commit to all the necessary ingredients for sustained success if their objective is to promote and embed changes in assessment practice. The ARIA project presented these ingredients as seven key processes as set out in Figure 1.1. Note that this schema is not

**Figure 1.1** Key processes in ensuring sustainable change

intended to imply that the change process in schools and education systems is simple and linear. The individual elements interact in a complex, interwoven and interdependent manner, though arguably there has to be an initial innovation to begin the process and the ultimate aim is arguably to ensure that the aims are sustainable. These processes are considered in the chapters that follow.

The second conclusion reached in ARIA was that another phenomenon was acting across the scene. This might be summarized as many voices seemingly talking about the same issue (improvement in assessment practice) while using almost as many definitions of that issue as there are voices. Ultimately, such a situation dissolves into a mêlée of jargon used to describe different types of assessment, different uses of assessment and different perceptions of what is considered to be acceptable quality in assessment practice. Not having an explicit view of what is 'good' assessment for any particular purpose has the knock-on effect of making it difficult to decide what an improvement is. Indeed, it is also difficult to propose what effective dissemination or professional development for good assessment practice might look like.

A set of principles and standards is therefore needed to guide the development of effective assessment practice. These should be designed to enable any stakeholder group to assess the extent to which they are effectively promoting and sustaining desirable changes in assessment and its use. As with the model of key processes above, the principles and standards put forward in this book have emerged from the studies of recent projects and from the series of expert seminars. These are set out in detail in Chapter 2.

## Structure

The book is presented in three parts and Part I: *Lighting the fuse* is designed to introduce the context of exciting change that is empowering teachers to add assessment skills to their repertoire of tools for improving pupils' learning. The chapters in this section therefore seek to ensure that readers are well prepared for dealing with what are sometimes quite complex concepts and practices. Following this introductory chapter, Chapter 1: *Assessment to support learning* covers the variety of purposes for assessment (including accountability), what teachers need to know about assessment and specifically the differences in purposes and usage that form the continuum between formative and summative assessment.

Following this, Chapter 2: *What is quality teacher assessment?* presents a synthesis of the insights and experiences of the 200-plus ARIA experts on a common language, in the form of principles and standards to guide assessment to improve learning in schools. Such an approach can also help to ensure that groups outside the school, such as advisory and inspection services, and policy makers, do not send contradictory messages on how assessment by teachers should develop.

The last chapter in the section, Chapter 3: *What's happening in the UK?* provides an overview of the recent curriculum-related assessment developments across the four main jurisdictions in the UK: England, Wales, Scotland and Northern Ireland. The analysis of the various policy developments confirms the widespread growth of teacher assessment and the many challenges still to be faced.

Part 2: *Spreading the word, widening the practice* begins the book's foray into understanding the complex processes involved in taking teacher assessment as a classroom innovation through to dynamically sustained practice. Chapter 4: *What is innovative about teacher assessment?* considers the concept of *innovation* in assessment and the importance of having evidence of teacher assessment being a viable and powerful classroom process (its '*warrant*'). Chapter 5: *Moving beyond the classroom* considers the various models of *dissemination* available for promoting teacher assessment on a wider basis than an individual teacher's classroom. The focus of the chapter is on the pursuit of 'transformation' of practice rather than mere 'transmission' of good practices.

Perhaps one of the most important chapters then follows – Chapter 6: *Professional learning to promote teacher assessment.* The chapter emphasizes the importance of facilitating teachers with time for personal reflection and sharing experiences, and enabling them to participate fully in the design of effective *professional learning* activities. The problems of a superficial grasp of the key issues in teacher assessment, the misleading allure of classroom strategies and a failure to harness teachers' beliefs and commitment are also exposed. Chapter 7: *Teachers as self-agents of change* completes Part 2 by stressing the importance of *agency*, and particularly that teachers must be at the forefront of changing their own practices. As in Chapter 6, notions of top-down and bottom-up are used to argue that teachers ultimately need more than information and guidance, or policy diktat, to undertake change. Their own needs and that of their pupils must generate their own intrinsic motivation to adopt and adapt new assessment practices in their classrooms.

Part 3: *Keeping it going* focuses on two important issues. The first, set out in Chapter 8: *Making a difference: evaluating the impact of innovations in assessment*, is that teachers and schools, and other interested parties, need to have a sound basis for believing that the changes are having an *impact*. Without this evidence of impact, there may be reluctance to maintain commitment and effort in the changes; indeed, there is every possibility that the teachers might query the point of doing it at all. Rather than simply perceiving there to be an impact, this chapter promotes a systematic approach to evaluating whether any changes are having the desired impact.

The final chapter, Chapter 9: *Embedding and sustaining developments in teacher assessment* is given over to the vital issue of ensuring that the changes in assessment practice are sustained. However, the key message here is that the needs of pupils, teachers and schools are constantly changing and that sustainability must therefore not be seen as a static situation. It is instead a dynamic concept, one that can only be secured if teachers are given the opportunity and encouragement to keep their assessment practices under review, as their needs and those of their pupils change over time.

## Using this book

Everyone involved in education, from teachers and schools through to policy makers, has to cooperate to ensure that desirable innovative practice is embraced and embedded throughout the system. Using this book, individual teachers and their schools as communities can develop, sustain and continually improve their assessment practices. In order to make the text immediately applicable in a school or local authority professional development setting, or in a higher education setting (e.g. Masters, PGCE, EdD), each end of chapter will offer a set of questions designed to prompt individual reflection and group discussion on the key issues concerned. In addition, a template for professional development workshops, which can address these types of question in the school, local authority or higher education context, is provided in Appendix 2. This proposes a 'snowball' format of individual refelction followed by discussion in pairs and foursomes, and provides suggestions on timing and approaches to enaging participants in discussions.

## Notes

1. Throughout the book we use pupil, student and learner interchange-
   ably, choosing the best fit with the context in each case.
2. The principles will be explained and developed in Chapter 2 – *What is
   quality teacher assessment?*
3. Analysis and Review of Innovations in Assessment – see Appendix 1
   for more details.

# Part I

# Lighting the fuse

# 1 Assessment to support learning

*Wynne Harlen and John Gardner*

This chapter provides an overview of the purposes and uses of classroom assessment by teachers or teacher assessment as it is better known (not to be confused with the assessment of teachers). At the heart of the matter lies the distinction between formative and summative uses of assessment information, and the basic argument that teacher assessment may be successfully used in both contexts. A primary aim of this chapter is therefore to clarify the often confusing terminology that misleadingly promotes the view that the method of assessment has to be exclusively formative or summative. School, i.e. is classroom-based teacher assessment is compared to external testing in terms of the different roles they play and the advantages and disadvantages they each have.

In 2007, Newton argued that assessment processes of different kinds may serve many purposes, in at least 22 categories that he illustrated in his paper. They included the familiar formative, diagnostic and qualifications-related uses along with less familiar variants such as placement, licensing and programme evaluation. In common with others in the field, he rejects the simplistic notion of an assessment being itself formative or summative, arguing that it is the purpose to which an assessment is put that is the crucial distinction. To try to limit inappropriate use of assessment information, he argues that anyone developing any form of assessment should identify the purposes for which it is fit and most importantly the purposes for which it is unfit: 'Stakeholders should be deprived of ignorance as an excuse for misuse' (Newton, 2007: 168).

There are strong demands for precise use of assessment terms in Newton's work and the nuances of meaning are well worth pursuing. However, we are interested here in the most practical of purposes, the use of assessment to support improved learning. Assessment by teachers in the classroom, that is, teacher assessment, has many purposes to which it can be put but our focus is on the most obvious: for helping pupils to learn and for contributing to judgements on pupils' progress and achievement.

## Purposes

The title of this chapter, *Assessment to support learning*, could well be taken to mean that it is about formative assessment, or assessment for learning. This purpose of assessment is now commonly accepted, if less widely practised than it is often assumed to be. It is sometimes contrasted with summative assessment, or assessment of learning, which serves the purpose of reporting on what has been learned at a particular time. These are the two main purposes of assessment and there are conflicting claims about how distinct they are in practice. For instance, in the view of Gipps (1994), 'Any attempt to use formative assessment for summative purposes will impair its formative role' (p. 14), while Black et al. (2003) advocate the use of summative tests to help learning. Certainly the study of current assessment practice leaves no doubt that summative assessment has an impact on learning but whether this is positive or negative depends on the use made of the information gathered in the assessment.

## Uses

In the case of formative assessment there is one main use for the information – to help learning. Assessment that does not do this simply cannot be called 'formative'. By contrast, information from summative assessments can have various uses. The two main uses fall under the headings: use of results for individual students and use of results for groups of students (classes, year groups, national populations). Within the school, individual students' assessment results may be used for record keeping, monitoring progress, reporting to parents, students and other teachers, and for career guidance. Summative assessment of individual students may also be used by agencies outside the school to select students or to award qualifications. Both of these uses directly affect the individual student to some degree. In addition, the aggregated results of summative assessments for groups of students are used both within and outside the school. Within the school they may be used for school self-evaluation, to monitor trends in performance or perhaps to evaluate the impact of changes in procedures or resource materials. Perhaps more controversially, aggregated results may also be used by agencies and authorities outside the school for:

- accountability – evaluation of teachers, schools, local authorities against targets;
- monitoring – students' average achievements within and across schools in particular areas, and across a whole system for year-on-year comparison.

Both of these external uses are problematic, particularly when the only information used is derived from test scores. Although the main focus of this book is assessment for uses relating to individual students, this use has to be seen against the background of the same data being used for accountability and particularly for creating performance targets and league tables of schools, as has been the practice in England since the introduction of national testing. As reported by Harlen and Deakin Crick (2003), this puts teachers under pressure to increase scores, which is widely recognized as leading to teaching to the tests, giving multiple practice tests and coaching pupils in how to answer test questions rather than in using and applying their understanding more widely. Other known consequences have been charted by the Assessment Reform Group (ARG, 2002a) as the demotivation of lower-achieving pupils and, for all pupils, a view of learning as product rather than process. It also leads to undue attention being focused on those who are performing just below the target level, with less attention for those who are either too far below or are already above the target level.

These effects are by now widely known and recognized by students themselves: 'Students are drilled to jump through hoops that the examiner is holding ... The mechanical exam process is moulding a mechanical education' (Tom Greene, a secondary school pupil, writing in *The Independent*, 17 August 2006) – and by parents:

> For my son, and for most 10-year-olds in the country, the next nine months will be ... a sterile, narrow and meaningless exercise in drilling and cramming. It's nothing to do with the skills of his teacher, who seems outstanding. Nor do I blame the school. It's called preparing for Key Stage 2 SATs.
>
> (Benaby, 2006)

as well as by teachers (NUT, 2006) and researchers.

For monitoring standards of pupil achievement at the regional or national levels, the interest is not in the performance of individual students but in the population performance in each learning domain, such as different aspects of mathematics, reading or other subjects. Thus, validity depends on how well the domain is sampled. If the data used in monitoring are derived from a summation of individual test results, as is the case in England where national tests results are used to monitor change in national standards, then the sample of the domain is restricted to the questions that any individual pupil can answer in a test of reasonable length. The questions do not necessarily represent a good sample of the domain, and will depend on the particular content of the test. Monitoring in this way does not provide sound information about changes in national levels of achievement, yet these are taken as measures of national 'standards' and important policy decisions are based on them.

We discuss the meaning of 'standards' in Chapter 2, but note here that a more valid approach to monitoring achievement levels would be to use a far greater number of items, providing a more representative sample of the domain. Since the concern is not with the performance of individual pupils, there is no need for all pupils to be given the same items. All that is needed is for each item to be attempted by an adequate sample of the population. Sampling of this kind, where only a small proportion of students is selected and each only takes a sample of the full range of items, is used in international surveys. These include the Programme for International Student Achievement (PISA) (OECD, 2009) and the Trends in International Mathematics and Science Study (TIMSS) (IEA, 2009) while national surveys include the Scottish Survey of Assessment (SSA) (SEED, 2005) and the older Assessment of Performance Unit (APU) for England, Wales and Northern Ireland (Foxman et al., 1991). As outlined in Chapter 3, there are emerging signs that the APU-like sampling strategy is being reconsidered for operation in England and Northern Ireland as a means of establishing national standards without burdening pupils unduly.

## Impact on learning

As mentioned in the introductory chapter and above, formative and summative assessment are not different kinds of assessment but do serve different purposes. Indeed, there is an argument that the terms 'formative assessment' and 'summative assessment' should not be used and should be replaced by 'assessment for formative purposes' and 'assessment for summative purposes'. However, so long as it is understood that the information from any assessment process has the potential to be used directly to help learning or simply to judge or record it, the former terms are useful in common parlance.

A teacher's mark or grade on a student's work may therefore end up simply as another entry in a record sheet or it may be used as a start of feedback to the student. For example, it could help with a pupil's future work by explaining the criteria used in arriving at the mark and identifying what aspects of the work were taken into account in the judgement. Hopefully, even the mark in the record book will also be used in a future review of the student's progress with a less direct, but still positive, role in providing for future learning. A student's participation in a national or international survey appears to have no possibility of improving that student's learning, but in the longer term the results of the survey should be used to improve the learning opportunities of other students, since the data collected make it possible to relate test results to the conditions of learning. If there is no prospect of the results being used to support learning, it is hard to understand why governments provide the quite considerable funding that such surveys require.

These arguments lead us to conclude that all assessment should ultimately improve learning, at the level of the individual student or through changes at the system level. This is one of the overarching principles that we develop in this book. It applies as much to assessment that is summative as to formative assessment, where it is a necessary requirement. The aim ought to be to conduct assessment for summative purposes in a way that supports the achievement of all learning goals and does not limit attention only to those learning outcomes and processes that are easy to assess. This is likely to mean that various ways of collecting assessment data are needed. Some outcomes, such as basic numeracy and literacy, may be quite adequately addressed by well-designed tests, but our concern here is with those that are not. When tests are favoured in government policies and are given high stakes by their use in setting targets and evaluating teachers and schools, the outcomes not adequately assessed by tests are in danger of being neglected in teaching.

## The formative role of assessment

When assessment is specifically intended to help learning, a simple check on its effectiveness would be to assess whether it leads to greater learning than would be the case when it is not being used. However, this is not a realistic criterion to use as it begs a number of questions about the nature of the learning, the period of time it covers and the competition with other influences on learning and so on. Indeed, it is not necessarily a straightforward matter to say whether the formative use of assessment is actually under way, given its complexity. Most projects aiming to improve formative assessment in normal classroom conditions do not provide research evidence that enables these questions to be adequately addressed.[1] Instead, the case for the importance of formative assessment can be made from arguments based on what is known about learning and from the evidence derived from controlled research studies, which show that improved learning follows when certain features of using assessment formatively are in place.

### Arguments based on learning

Current views of learning emphasize the importance of the active role of learners in developing their understanding through using existing ideas and skills to build 'bigger' ideas and more advanced skills. 'Big' ideas are ones that can be applied in different contexts; they enable learners to understand a wide range of phenomena by identifying the essential links ('meaningful patterns' as Bransford et al., 1999, put it) between different situations without being diverted by superficial features. Merely memorizing facts or a fixed set of procedures does not support this ability to apply learning to contexts beyond the ones in which it was learned. Knowledge that is understood is therefore useful knowledge that can be used in problem-solving and decision-making.

The teacher's role in this learning is to make provision for appropriate experiences that challenge students' existing ideas and skills but are not out of their reach. It means that teachers take steps to find out what sense students are making of their learning activities. Particular kinds of 'deep' questioning are important here and students need to have opportunities to reflect, discuss and consider thoughtful answers to such questions. The information gathered by teachers has to be fed back to students and used to regulate teaching so that the pace of moving towards learning goals is adjusted to ensure the engagement and active participation of the students. Students can participate in these processes if teachers communicate to them their goals for the lesson and the criteria by which they can judge their progress towards the goals. The lesson goals may well vary in detail for different students according to their previous experience and progress in their learning.

It follows, then, that some of the key features of the formative use of assessment are likely to be that:

- information about ongoing learning is used in decisions about the pace and content of teaching;
- teachers ask questions that enable them to know about the developing ideas, skills and attitudes of their students;
- students are provided with feedback in a form that helps them engage with further learning;
- students take an active part in their learning and participate in deciding the goals to which they are working;
- students understand the quality criteria to be applied to their work and so can take part in self- and peer-assessment.

## Research evidence

These points emerge from considering how learning with understanding takes place and reflect closely the features of classroom assessment that research has found to improve learning. Indeed, there is a large and growing body of evidence that formative assessment improves learning. Empirical investigations of classroom assessment have been the subject of several reviews of research, principally those by Natriello (1987), Kulik and Kulik (1987), Crooks (1988), Black (1993) and Black and Wiliam (1998a). The last of these has attracted a good deal of attention world-wide for several reasons. For example, its dissemination in the form of a short booklet, *Inside the Black Box* (Black and Wiliam, 1998b), meant it has reached a much greater audience than would a research journal article. In addition, the authors' quantification of the positive impact on learning, of using assessment for learning (AfL), made compelling reading. They estimated that the gains in learning were large enough to 'improve performances of pupils in GCSE by between one and two grades' (Black and Wiliam, 1998b: 4). Further, they reported that 'improved formative assessment helps the (so-called) low attainers more than the rest, and so reduces the spread of attainment whilst also raising it overall' (ibid). This means of expressing the impact of AfL was more effective in communicating with policy makers than providing evidence in the conventional academic manner.

Black et al. (2003) cite research by Bergan et al. (1991), White and Frederiksen (1998) and the review of Fuchs and Fuchs (1986) as providing evidence of better learning when teachers take care to review information about students and to use it to guide their teaching. Butler (1988), for example, showed the importance of non-judgemental feedback in the form of comments with no marks. Schunk (1996) also found positive impacts on achievement as a result of students' self-assessment. These all reflect a view of learning in which students participate actively rather than being passive receivers of knowledge. This means that assessment, which is used to help learning, plays a particularly important part in the achievement of the kinds of goal of understanding and thinking valued in education for the twenty-first century.

## Extent and quality of practice

The practice of using assessment to help learning is a complex combination of interconnected features as listed above. However, no study to date has attempted to combine all the aspects of formative assessment that have been the subject of separate studies. It is therefore not clear just how important it is for all features to be in place for the benefits to be realized. Taking on change in the full range of practices is likely to be overwhelming and most teachers begin by choosing one or two changes, such as in questioning or procedures for feedback to students. More information is needed to confirm whether this selective approach can be regarded as effective formative use of assessment.

What is already clear, however, is that positive impacts may not result if teachers are following procedures mechanically without understanding their purpose. For example, Smith and Gorard (2005) reported that when some teachers put comments but no marks on students' work (a key feature of the formative use of assessment), these students made less progress than others given marks. Most notably, however, the majority of the teachers' comments illustrated by Smith and Gorard merely commented on how well the students had done and did not supply guidance on how to improve the work. Almost a year later, after a systematically more thorough programme of introducing AfL, including support for written feedback, the assistant head of the same school was reporting that Key Stage 3 results for English, mathematics and science had steadily improved (Burns, 2006). It is essential, therefore, for teachers to understand the underlying rationale for any new approach, and to embrace the change in teacher – student relationships that is involved in using assessment to help learning. Without this change, students will not use feedback to improve their work or to reveal their understanding and difficulties, as is necessary for assessment to be used for learning. This example underlines the point that it is necessary to distinguish between bringing about change in assessment practice and bringing about change that is consistent with improving engagement in learning. It also emphasizes that such change will not happen without specific support to help the teachers to assimilate the underlying rationale for the change.

There is, therefore, a matter of quality of practice to be considered, which involves a general change in the relationship between teacher and students. Wiliam et al. (2004) quote Brousseau (1984) who describes this as renegotiating the 'learning contract' between teachers and students. This refers to the shift in responsibility for learning from belonging only to the teacher to being shared with students. As Harlen (2006) has argued, openness in relation to assessment also provides the context for assessment evidence, gathered and used as part of teaching, to be the basis for the summative role of assessment of learning outcomes relating to all learning goals.

## The summative role of assessment

### The impact of assessment

There is a good deal of evidence to support the claim that outcomes that are assessed are the ones that are given most attention in teaching, particularly when high stakes are attached to the results. Harlen and Deakin Crick (2003) have shown that setting targets in terms of test results, with sanctions attached to failure to meet the targets, leads to a range of practices that narrow students' learning experiences and affect their motivation for learning. In James et al.'s (2006a) study, evidence from 1,500 staff in 40 primary and secondary schools in England led to the conclusion that there is no doubt that teachers are teaching to the tests their pupils have to take; they do not feel they can do anything else. Marshall and Drummond's (2006) case studies confirmed this view, revealing that teachers believed that 'there are circumstances beyond their control which inhibit their ability to teach in a way they understand to be good practice' (p. 147). These 'circumstances' are the tests, which cannot, on account of their form and length, adequately assess certain important learning outcomes. Learning experiences that lead to deep understanding are unlikely to receive the attention that matches the rhetoric of such learning unless it is included in the assessment that matters.

## The limitations of tests

The primary reason that these learning outcomes are not currently included in the assessment of learning outcomes that 'matter' relates to the difficulty of assessing them through the methods that are presently favoured. For assessment where the results are used beyond the school, tests are preferred because they are considered to be of high reliability and to be 'fair'. In this sense, reliability refers to whether the result would have come out differently on a different occasion for the same student assessed on the same learning outcomes. However, as the work of Wiliam (2001), Black and Wiliam (2006), and Gardner and Cowan (2005) has demonstrated, even if every item were to be free of ambiguity and could be marked without error, there is still an unavoidable error in the overall test score. For example, error is introduced when the items included are a selection of possible choices and a different selection could produce a different result. In practice, items can never be error-free and the steps taken to raise reliability favour items that are 'closed', that is, having fixed responses. Their marking then depends as little as possible on human judgement. Clearly, items that require students to be creative, present arguments or show understanding of a complex situation do not fit this description and appear less frequently in current tests than they ought to. Even when such items are included, high stakes add pressure that leads to teaching how to pass tests rather than spending time helping students to understand what is being tested. As Harlen and Deakin Crick have argued:

> Direct teaching on how to pass the tests can be very effective, so much so that Gordon and Reese (1997) concluded that students can pass tests 'even though the students have never learned the concepts on which they are being tested'. As teachers become more adept at this process, they can even teach students to answer

correctly test items intended to measure students' ability to apply, or synthesize, even though the students have not developed application, analysis or synthesis skills. Not only is the scope and depth of learning seriously undermined, but this also affects the validity of the tests, for they no longer indicate that the students have the knowledge and skill needed to answer the questions correctly.

(Harlen and Deakin Crick, 2003: 199)

As implied here, validity refers to how well the assessment reflects the achievements that it is intended to assess. If students are under so much pressure that they feel anxiety due to the high stakes associated with their performance, they may not perform as well as they are able. This may act to reduce the validity of the test. The extent to which an assessment is capable of capturing the achievements intended can be established by expert judgement – for instance in comparing the content of the tasks assessed with the content of the curriculum or course it is designed to assess – or by statistical examination of consistency in the results. However, the concept of validity is rather more complex than this, particularly because it will depend on the use made of the results. For instance, an examination result may be reasonably valid for assessing achievement as a result of a course, but less so for predicting achievement in further courses. In order to decide the most valid data for a particular use, it is necessary to consider the needs and points of view of those who use the information.

## The potential of tests

It is worth noting that valid items assessing such outcomes as problem-solving, enquiry skills and critical thinking can be created but, because the response to them is highly dependent on the choice of content, a large number of items is needed to obtain a reliable score. Thus, they can be used in surveys where every individual does not need to take every item. Some items of these types were included in surveys conducted nationally by the APU in England, Wales and Northern Ireland in the 1980s. They also currently feature in the National Assessment of Educational Progress (NAEP) in the United States and the Scottish Survey of Achievement (SEED, 2005). The items in these surveys are not limited to what can be assessed on paper and include, for example, assessment of listening and speaking and performance of investigations in science and mathematics. As they are designed to monitor performance of a population in a particular learning domain, the results have no significance for individual students or even classes and schools. They are, therefore, low stakes and there is no incentive to teach to what is being tested. The influence of the test content is at the conceptual level of the test framework, not in relation to specific items. As Kellaghan (1996) argues, most learning from the surveys is at the system level where the results do not inform policy makers solely about performance and trends in performance across a range of aspects within each domain tested. They also provide information about how factors such as curricula, time spent on school work, teacher training and class size are found to be associated with variation in student achievement.

## Possibilities offered by teacher assessment

Returning to the matter of assessing individual students, it is evident that tests of any reasonable length are not reliable or valid for assessing certain learning outcomes. In particular, they are not suited to assessing some of the essential elements of twenty-first-century education such as problem-solving, critical thinking, enterprise and citizenship. Valid assessment would require students to be in situations where they can demonstrate these attributes when they are assessed; faced with real problems and required to link one experience with another. An alternative to written tests is clearly needed if we are to include these outcomes in summative assessment. It can be found in using the judgements of the teacher, acknowledging that the experience students need in order to develop the desired skills, understanding and attitudes also provide opportunities for progress towards these outcomes to be assessed. Assessment by teachers can take evidence from regular activities, supplemented if necessary by evidence from specially devised tasks; that is, introduced specifically to provide opportunities for students to use the skills and understanding to be assessed.

Over the period of time for which achievement is being reported (a term or half year for regular reports to parents and one or more years for external certification), students have opportunities to engage in a number of activities in which a range of attributes can be developed. These same activities also provide opportunities for the development to be assessed by the teacher. In other words, the limitation of the restricted time that a test provides does not apply when assessment is teacher-based.

Teachers' assessments are often perceived as having low reliability but the evidence for this comes from situations and studies where no moderation or other form of quality assurance has been in place. Clearly, some quality assurance of the process of arriving at judgements is necessary, particularly when the results are used for decisions that affect students' future learning opportunities. According to Harlen (2004), when steps are taken to moderate the results, the reliability of teachers' judgements is comparable with that of tests. Moreover, the moderation process is itself widely recognized as being a valuable form of professional learning. For example, Maxwell, referring to experience in Queensland, comments that:

> The most powerful means for developing professional competence in assessment is the establishment of regular professional conversations among teachers about student performance (moderation conversations). This is best focussed on actual examples of student portfolios.
>
> (Maxwell, 2004: 7)

### Advantages of teacher assessment

There are three further advantages of using teachers' judgements for the summative use of assessment. The first is that it enables processes of learning as well as outcomes to be assessed. Such information is particularly useful where the ability to undertake further learning is of interest. For example, for those who select students for advanced vocational or academic courses of study, it is as important to know if candidates have developed the skills and desire for learning, that is, if they have 'learned how to learn' and are likely to benefit from further study.

The second advantage is that using teachers' judgements opens the possibility of students playing some part in the assessment of their learning outcomes for summative purposes. This requires that they know the criteria by which their work is judged, taking away the mystery and anxiety often associated with some assessment procedures. The criteria ought to be progressive so that students see not only what they have achieved but what they have still to achieve. Students need also to be made aware of the purpose of the assessment and how it can help them to recognize their strengths and where they need to make more effort. This enables the process of arriving at a summative judgement to be used formatively by students, who see what they have to aim for in the longer term, and by teachers as feedback into planning.

The third advantage is that evidence collected and used formatively can be used for summative purposes when judged against the standards for reporting students' levels of achievement. The mechanism for doing this, however, must take account of the differences in the nature of the judgements made for formative and for summative purposes. Evidence collected and used formatively is detailed, relates to specific lesson goals and will be used to give positive feedback. It takes into account the particular circumstances of individual students and assists in making judgements about next steps in learning. It leads to action and not grades or levels. For summative use, the evidence from formative assessment needs to be brought together and judged against the criteria that indicate the various grades or levels used in reporting. Thus, the evidence can be used for two purposes, with the proviso for summative use that it is reinterpreted against the same reporting criteria for all students. This involves finding the 'best fit' between the evidence gathered about each student and the reporting levels. In this process the change over time can be taken into account so that preference is given to evidence that shows progress during the period covered by the summary judgement or report.

## Conclusion

Externally generated and marked tests and tasks have important roles to play in schools, for example, in helping teachers to benchmark their understanding of levels of performance. However, their use for supporting learning is less obvious. More contentious uses such as school and teacher evaluation do render them problematic in a variety of disruptive ways such as their impact on what is taught, the targets they give rise to and the burdens of anxiety and time that they may place on the learning process.

In contrast, teacher assessment comprises a large collection of information gleaned from the daily classroom interactions between pupils and teachers, and between pupils and pupils. The interactions cover many different types of process including the dynamic assessments of questioning and feedback, the reflective assessments of self- and peer-assessment, the sharing of learning goals and the criteria that indicate their achievement, and the long-term progression-related evidence from pupils' work. Such a wealth of evidence is primarily used in an *ad hoc* support of learning 'in the moment' (assessments for formative purposes) but can also be captured in suitable forms for reporting progress and performance (assessment for summative judgements). As Brooks and Tough put it:

> The most effective schools now practise a culture of continuous teacher-led assessment, appraisal and adjustment of teaching practices to personalise learning for all their pupils. It seems clear that assessment that does not assist the learning of the child is of very limited value, and in many ways the certification of achievement and the accountability role of assessment are only important because of their links to this.
>
> (Brooks and Taylor: 2006)

**Questions for reflection**

1. In what contexts is it important or not important that classroom-based teacher assessment should be made as reliable and valid as possible? What are the reasons for this?

2. Why does our education system require summative judgements to be made on pupil progress and performance? Does this requirement compromise the use of assessment to support learning?

3. What might be the arguments for and against the use of surveys to provide information at a national level?

4. What might a system look like where all assessment supported learning?

# Note

1. The work on outcomes of the King's Medway Oxfordshire Formative Assessment project (KMOFAP) reported by Wiliam et al. (2004) is an exception. See Chapter 8.

# 2 What is quality teacher assessment?

*Wynne Harlen*

This chapter discusses the properties of assessment practice that are considered to indicate quality. These relate to the impact that assessment has on learning and the consequent need to ensure that all learning goals are included as validly as possible and as reliably as necessary for purpose. They also cover the help given to users of assessment to understand the reasons for and methods of assessment, including its unavoidable inaccuracy, the role of students in assessing their own work and the importance of using a variety of methods to ensure that all students have the opportunity to show what they can do. From this discussion we identify 10 principles, expressed broadly as applying to national policy as much as to classroom practice. The tenth principle, that assessment methods and procedures should meet agreed standards of quality in practice, leads to a discussion of the meaning of standards and of the value judgements involved in identifying them. The purpose of such standards is to support critical review of assessment plans and procedures and to propose directions for change to improve practice. A set of standards of quality is then proposed in relation to formative and summative assessment applying to the practice of teachers in the classroom, managers in schools, local advisers or inspectors and national policy makers.

## Introduction

When we seek to improve any practice – in the present case, assessment practice – it is necessary to have a view of what we mean by quality, otherwise there is no basis for identifying improvement. The ultimate aim of all change and innovation in education is to improve learning and, as argued briefly in Chapter 1, we consider that all assessment, formative and summative, should benefit learning either directly or indirectly and so raise standards. But this raises questions such as: *What kind of learning?* and *Standards in what?* Inevitably, answers to these questions involve judgements about the learning that is valued, the balance between learning 'the basics' and the development of higher level thinking and understanding of what it is to learn (the 'new basics'), and the role of schooling in the overall education of students.

This chapter attempts to explain how teachers and others may identify 'good' formative and summative assessment practice, not in terms of identifying effective practices, of which there are many, but in terms of the standards that effective practices ought to meet. These standards may be met in a variety of ways to suit particular circumstances. As well as being based on evidence from practice, they reflect the kind of learning outcome and processes that are valued and ought to be facilitated by assessment that is judged to be effective. The arguments on which the decisions about the standards are based reflect certain principles, which we discuss and identify in the first part of this chapter. We then clarify the meaning being given to 'standards' in this context and set out some standards of quality for assessment practice that apply to the classroom, the school, the local authority and national policy.

## Principles of assessment practice

One of the key insights from the ARIA project was that a lack of an explicit view on what 'good' assessment is has the effect of making it difficult to decide what an improvement is or indeed what effective dissemination or professional development for good assessment practice might look like. Drawing on the experience of the 200+ experts involved in the study, and the analysis of the selection of major teacher assessment initiatives, sets of principles and standards were developed to address the concept of quality in assessment. There were 10 principles in all and these are listed for convenience here:

1. Assessment of any kind should ultimately improve learning.
2. Assessment methods should enable progress in all important learning goals to be facilitated and reported.
3. Assessment procedures should include explicit processes to ensure that information is valid and is as reliable as necessary for its purpose.
4. Assessment should promote public understanding of learning goals relevant to students' current and future lives

5. Assessment of learning outcomes should be treated as approximations, subject to unavoidable errors.
6. Assessment should be part of a process of teaching that enables students to understand the aims of their learning and how the quality of their achievement will be judged.
7. Assessment methods should promote the active engagement of students in their learning and its assessment.
8. Assessment should enable and motivate students to show what they can do.
9. Assessment should combine information of different kinds, including students' self-assessments, to inform decisions about students' learning and achievements.
10. Assessment methods should meet standards that reflect a broad consensus on quality at all levels from classroom practice to national policy.

Each of these principles is presented and developed in the sections below with the descriptions of the standards then following.

## Principle 1: Assessment of any kind should ultimately improve learning

The role of assessment in supporting learning is obvious in the case of the formative use of assessment, where the whole purpose is to assist learning. Assessment that does not do this cannot be called 'formative'. It is perhaps less obvious in the case of the summative use of assessment, where the purpose is to inform students, teachers, parents and others of what has been achieved. Nevertheless, the aim ought to be to conduct assessment for summative purposes in a way that supports and does not inhibit the learning. The concern here, therefore, is mainly with the summative assessment that teachers carry out for uses within and external to the school and which may have unintended negative impact on learning.

The impact of assessment will depend on how frequently and in what manner it is used as well as on the information that is gathered and how it in turn is used. It is claimed that frequent testing, where tests are tailored to progress, can have a positive impact on learning. Such programmes generally concern the formation of basic skills that depends on repeated practice if they are to become automatic. But Harlen and Deakin Crick (2003) have shown that assessment carried out frequently for the purpose of grading, whether it is by testing or other means, can have unwanted consequences for students' motivation for learning, their self-esteem, effort and achievement. Reay and Wiliam (1999) have reported that the feedback students receive from frequent grading or 'levelling' of their work is predominantly judgemental, encouraging competition and comparison with each other, which is demotivating for those who are constantly judged as lower achieving. An increase in the incidence of classroom testing is associated with high stakes external testing since this makes many teachers feel compelled to give students numerous practice tests. ARG (2006) has also argued that the amount of time spent on practising tests in the months preceding national testing can seriously reduce time for learning, which itself can negatively impact on learning, quite apart from undermining enjoyment of school experience.

These negative effects of testing make a case for considering alternatives, to serving the purposes of summative assessment, that will have a more positive impact. There is ample evidence that this is possible. For example, Harlen (2007) quotes a study in the USA in a school district that agreed to waive standardized testing for two years in the participating schools. In this study, Flexer et al. (1995) conducted weekly workshops with teachers to introduce them to assessing students' performance instead of using tests. The researchers reported several effects on teachers and on students by the end of the first year. Teachers were using more hands-on activities and problem-solving and were asking students for explanations. They were also trying to use more systematic observations for assessment. All agreed that the students had learned more and that they knew more about what their students knew. The teachers reported generally positive feedback from their own classes and the students had better conceptual understanding, could solve problems better and explain solutions. The teachers' response was to become more convinced of the benefit of such changes and to attempt further change in assessment and instruction practices.

Hall et al. (1997) have shown that when national curriculum assessment was first introduced in England, teacher assessment, based on judgements across a range of students' work, was perceived by the teachers in their project sample as having a positive impact on students' learning. The impact was enhanced by teachers working collaboratively towards shared understanding of the goals and the procedures for achieving these goals. However, Hall and Harding (2002) later found that the funding and opportunities for these meetings had declined in the face of pressure to raise test scores and the ground that was gained in the quality of teachers' assessment in the early and mid-1990s was lost.

This experience clearly points to the importance of taking the impact of assessment into account in national policy as well as classroom practice. Some evidence of this in the formulation of new assessment policy in

Wales was recorded during the ARIA expert seminars and concluded that assessment that exists primarily to provide data about attainment, without due regard to the need to benefit the learner and learning, is not worth doing.

## Principle 2: Assessment methods should enable progress in all important learning goals to be facilitated and reported

Some skills, knowledge and understandings are more easily assessed than others. Given the undeniable truth that what is assessed will be taught, it is essential that the assessment methods used are capable of assessing the full range of goals considered to be important in the twenty-first century. In terms of what is learned, current thinking world-wide emphasizes the importance of helping students to develop types of skill, attitude and understanding that are regarded as more important than accumulating large amounts of factual knowledge. Facts can be found readily from the information sources widely available through the Internet. What are needed are the skills to access these sources and the understanding to select what is relevant and to make sense of it. In making these claims, however, it is important to emphasize the difference between factual knowledge of isolated pieces of information and knowledge that is essential to understanding and indeed to the development of skills and attitudes. The skills will include, but go beyond, basic numeracy and literacy and will involve knowledge – procedural knowledge, the knowledge of 'how to do something' in contrast with propositional knowledge, the knowledge of something. The continued importance of basic numeracy and literacy is not denied by acknowledging that they are far from sufficient for modern life and that the 'new basics' of problem-solving, critical and creative thinking, learning how to learn, and so on must be given at least as much attention.

Students also need broad, widely applicable concepts and the ability to use them to solve problems and make decisions in new situations. This is often expressed in terms of becoming 'literate', meaning in this context the ability to engage effectively with different aspects of modern life. So it is common to refer to 'technological literacy', 'mathematical literacy', 'scientific literacy', even 'political and social literacy'. Being literate in these various respects indicates having the knowledge and skills that are needed by everyone, not just those who will be specialists in or make a career in one of these areas. The emphasis is not on mastering a body of knowledge but on having, and being able to use, a general understanding of the main or key ideas in making informed decisions and participating in society. Literacy, as used in these ways, does not mean reading and writing *about* technology, mathematics, science, and so on. Rather, it means having the understanding and skills to participate in the discussion of issues and to make decisions in the many challenges in everyday life that involve technology, science, politics, and so on.

Facing new challenges will be the normal run of things rather than the exception in the future lives of young people, as changes in technology affecting everyday life occur at an ever-increasing rate. Dealing with challenges responsibly involves a broad understanding of society and democratic processes and some experience in participating in them. These are among the aims of citizenship education. Being able to manage change, and do more than respond to problems, requires creativity and enterprise, which are important features in current views of what the curriculum should include. Underlying all attempts to prepare students for meeting change with confidence is surely the need for them to learn with understanding and to learn how to learn.

Understanding frequently occurs in the expression of learning goals, but often with little real attention given to it. Taken seriously, the development of understanding has strong implications for curriculum content, pedagogy and assessment. Understanding shows in the ability to organize knowledge, to relate it actively to new and to past experience, forming 'big' ideas, much in the way that Bransford et al. (1999) distinguish 'experts' from 'novices'. In order for these abilities to be assessed, therefore, students should be in situations as close as possible to reality, where they need to make decisions, solve problems, and so on. This has implications for how teachers teach as well as how students learn.

Views on how learning with understanding takes place emphasize the importance of what students already know and can do. Learners use their existing ideas and skills to make sense of new experience and in the process new knowledge may or may not be constructed. Several factors within the learning environment influence whether or not learning takes place. These include the:

- size of the step between current ideas and what is needed to make sense of new experience;
- support (scaffolding) given in using new concepts and linking them to existing ones;
- feedback given about progress towards learning goals;
- opportunities for students to share their own and others' ways of making sense of new experiences.

All these factors can support or, in their absence, inhibit the processes of recognizing new patterns or new ways of looking at things that make more sense than their earlier ideas. The learners' roles are to be active in generating their own understanding.

Recognizing that it is the students who do the learning, the role of teachers is to provide access to information and alternative ideas, and support and experiences for students to develop their ideas and thinking. The conditions for learning include not only the opportunities for students to encounter ideas, materials and phenomena relevant to particular domains of learning, but also opportunities to:

- face challenging tasks, with appropriate scaffolding, that will advance thinking;
- link new experiences and information to their existing ideas and skills;
- talk about their ideas and what they are learning;
- assess what and how they have learned;
- reflect critically on the learning process.

Providing these learning opportunities clearly requires teachers to collect and use information about students' existing ideas and skills and therefore to be in situations where they need to be used. The inclusion of talk reflects the emphasis it is given in recent accounts of learning. Alexander (2004) spells this out in identifying the concept of dialogic teaching, described as 'a distinct pedagogical approach', in which 'teaching harnesses the power of talk to stimulate and extend children's thinking, and to advance their learning and understanding' (p. 1). Dialogic teaching contrasts with teaching where the exchange between teacher and students is one-sided, with the teacher being the source of information and dominating the questioning.

Alexander (2004) also points out that dialogic teaching 'enables the teacher more precisely to diagnose and assess' (p. 1), making clear that the process is very similar to that of formative assessment. It aims to engage children and teachers in listening carefully and responding to each other, asking and answering questions, expressing, explaining and evaluating ideas, arguing and justifying them. In this process teachers can both gain and use information about how students' learning is progressing.

## Principle 3: Assessment procedures should include explicit processes to ensure that information is valid and is as reliable as necessary for its purpose

Harlen (2007) argues that the properties of assessment that need to be considered in relation to fitness for purpose should include validity, reliability, impact and cost in terms of use of time and other resources. The concern here is with the first two; validity being taken to mean how well what is assessed corresponds with the behaviours or learning outcomes that are intended to be assessed, and reliability being the consistency or accuracy of the results, often measured by the extent to which the assessment gives the same results if repeated. Various kinds of validity have been identified, including what Messick (1989) refers to as consequential validity, which we have discussed under 'impact'. Here the focus is on construct validity, referring to what is assessed.

A key factor concerning validity and reliability in assessment is that in practice these properties are not independent of each other. Rather, they interact in a way that makes it impossible to change one without affecting the other. For instance, efforts to increase the reliability of a test mean that the sample of items included will favour those that can be most consistently marked. This is likely to mean more items requiring only factual knowledge and in a closed format (multiple choice or short answer), and to exclude those that require application of knowledge and more open-ended tasks. The consequent limitation on what is covered in a test affects its validity; increasing reliability decreases validity. Attempts to increase validity by widening the range of items, say, by including more open-response items where more judgement is needed in marking, will mean that the reliability is reduced. If teachers' assessment is used, validity may be high since the data can include all the learning goals, but reliability will be low unless steps are taken to moderate the judgements. However, there is then a danger that moderation procedures lead teachers to confine their attention to aspects where they can be most confident of their judgements, thus restricting validity.

Thus, there is always a trade-off between validity and reliability. Where the balance is struck depends on the purpose of the assessment. For formative assessment validity is paramount; the assessment must address all goals if it is to help learning. However, while accuracy is clearly a desirable property of any information, it is not necessary to be overconcerned about the reliability of formative assessment information because it is gathered frequently and the teacher will be able to use feedback to correct for a mistaken judgement. In the case of summative assessment for internal purposes, the trade-off can also be in favour of validity, since no terminal decisions need hang on the reported data. This would suggest that use of teachers' judgements based on the full range of work is to be preferred to tests. If the evidence is derived from regular work and is gathered over a period of time, it covers a range of opportunities for students to show their learning without the anxiety associated with tests, which reduces validity.

For purposes external to the school, and particularly where high stakes are attached to the results for either the individual students or for the teacher, accuracy is of central importance. The assumption that tests and examinations are necessarily more accurate than teachers' judgements leaves two important points out of the account. The first is that when criteria are well specified and understood, teachers are able to make judgements of acceptable reliability. The second is the error that arises because tests are limited to only a small sample of the work covered and a different selection of items could easily produce a different result for particular students. For example, Wiliam (2001) and Black and Wiliam (2006) estimated that, in the case of the national tests at age 14 in England, even if the measured reliability of the test is high at 0.85, about 40 per cent of students will be awarded the wrong grade level. The extent of misclassification has recently been challenged by Newton (2009) but the central argument remains that the results from tests can be significantly inaccurate in relation to a student's expected level of attainment. When teachers' judgements are used, taking evidence from across the whole range of work, this source of misclassification is removed.

## Principle 4: Assessment should promote public understanding of learning goals relevant to students' current and future lives

Schools do not exist in isolation; they both serve and respond to the needs of society. Outside the school there are users of assessment, including parents, school governors or their equivalent, employers and staff of further and higher education, who often bring pressure to bear on school policies. There are also other members of the public who exercise their views about education through the ballot box. Members of school management teams also use assessment of learning outcomes as part of the evidence for school self-evaluation and improvement planning.

Assessment of students' achievement is the form in which many of these users, particularly those external to the school, receive information about education. It is clearly important to ensure that changes in schools are not restrained either by external users' outdated views of the goals of learning and of what is appropriate assessment, or by assumptions of those within the school about the information external users want. Thus, deliberate steps need to be taken to ensure two-way communication, so that changes in assessment practice are made when necessary and the reasoning and evidence for changes are clear to all involved. A key feature of this communication should be openness about the pros and cons of different methods of assessment and their suitability for assisting the achievement and reporting of the learning goals of twenty-first-century education.

## Principle 5: Assessment of learning outcomes should be treated as approximations, subject to unavoidable errors

Part of the understanding of assessment should be the realization that it is inherently inaccurate. Any measurement is subject to error, even that of physical properties such as length or weight, but the error is greater in the case of educational assessment for a variety of reasons. For a start what is measured can only be an outward sign of something that cannot be directly observed – the processes going on inside the heads of learners. Then there is constant change in what is measured. We expect students to be making progress, so they present a moving target. In addition, the process of assessment has unavoidable errors. In the case of tests, Black and Wiliam (2002) identify the main sources of possible error as arising from:

- variation in a pupil's performance according to the particular items chosen for test;
- pupils performing better or worse on different days on the same test;
- marks awarded for the same answer varying from one marker to another.

The first type is unavoidable in tests and arises because a large number of possible items could be included in a test for a curriculum domain. Test developers take pains to ensure that a particular selection is a balanced sample of the pool of possible items. Nevertheless, the sample in a test is not the same as the whole range of items, and pupils will respond differently to different samples: the shorter the duration of the test, the larger the sampling error. The error may be much larger than is generally realized (see Wiliam, 2001). It could be reduced by having a longer test, providing a larger sample of the item pool, but the gain is not in proportion to the test length. For instance, Wiliam (2001) has argued that a test of about 30 hours would be needed to reduce the misclassification in Key Stage 2 national curriculum assessments (commonly known as Sats[1]) from 40 to 10 per cent.

The second type of error above is also unavoidable in tests such as the Sats, which take place at given times. It can only be reduced by spreading the testing over several occasions. The third source of error can be reduced by refining and checking marking, as much as resources allow, and selecting items so that less judgement is needed (which is likely to infringe validity). This source of unreliability can never be completely eliminated as long as human beings are involved. The first and second of these errors apply to some extent to teachers' judgements, for they too can be selective in what they pay attention to, and may vary in how they use criteria in making judgements.

The implications of these points is not that all tests and all assessments are worthless but that we should understand the limitations of the results and interpret them accordingly, recognizing that good assessment can do no more than give a good approximation of students' achievements. Moreover, we should try to avoid the need to make distinctions between students that are based on differences smaller than the margin of error of the measure used. However, when distinctions have to be made, the understanding of the students themselves of how their achievements match up to the standards required, as discussed below, can avoid total dependence on tests or judgements by others.

## Principle 6: Assessment should be part of a process of teaching that enables students to understand the aims of their learning and how the quality of their achievements will be judged

## Principle 7: Assessment methods should promote the active engagement of students in their learning and its assessment

These two principles cover issues relating to the role of students in assessment for formative use, a notion that is integral to using assessment for learning (AfL). The kind of learning discussed earlier is not a matter of absorbing information and ready-made ideas, but involves the active participation of learners in making sense of new experiences. They must be willing to make the effort necessary to do this. Knowing what to aim for and when they are making progress is central to the motivation to continue. So students need to know the goals of their work and how to go about achieving them. Perhaps, surprisingly, students are frequently unable to articulate what their teacher intends them to learn from an activity, as opposed to what they are supposed to do.

To take responsibility for improving their work, students also need to know how quality or 'good work' is identified. This is often best communicated through examples and discussion of what makes, for instance, a good project report or a good scientific investigation. The importance of knowing the criteria for judging their work applies as much in summative assessment as in using assessment to help learning. Students as well as parents need to understand the criteria used in summarizing and reporting their achievements. This is central to demystifying summative assessment and an important step in reducing its negative impact.

A good deal of the emotion that is aroused by summative assessment comes from a fear or suspicion of the unknown. Students and teachers know full well that there is a lottery in the selection of questions for any test, since it cannot encompass all parts of what has been studied. To take the fear and suspicion away from summative assessment, it is necessary to be completely open about the need for and purpose of assessment and why it is carried out in particular ways. Those most closely involved ought to be fully aware of how evidence is gathered and how judgements are made. Even the youngest students can be given some explanation of what evidence they and their teachers can use to judge whether they are making progress. The more open we are about assessment procedures, the easier it is for students to assess their own work, so that there are no surprises (for students or parents) in the reports of the level reached at a particular time. When students and parents expect teachers to be the only ones to say how students are doing, it will take time to establish a different, more collaborative relationship.

## Principle 8: Assessment should enable and motivate students to show what they can do

Using AfL in accordance with principles 6 and 7 means that students understand what they have to do to achieve their immediate goal and can work towards it in the confidence that they can succeed. Formative assessment ensures that the steps are ones they can take. When assessment is used to summarize learning, however, how can the same feelings of confidence and satisfaction in achievement be assured? The problem arises when tests are used, for they inevitably bring uncertainty about what will be required. Using teachers' judgements can bring a different kind of uncertainty about how performance is judged and may be a cause of anxiety for the students, even though the tasks are part of the regular work and are known to them. Several steps can be taken in both cases.

Following from the discussion of openness, it is important for students to know as much as possible about the tasks and the criteria to be used. This may seem to be an invitation to practise test taking, but there is a considerable difference between knowing what taking a test involves and being drilled in how to answer specific questions. It is important to avoid the anxiety of the unknown, which is a cause of error in the results and unfairness to individuals as well as threatening students' feelings about themselves as learners. The type of feedback that students receive on their work as part of classroom assessment should ensure that they understand how it is being judged when grades and levels have to be assigned. The use of formative assessment should ensure that students experience success in their work, which motivates effort in further tasks.

When grades and levels have to be assigned for the purpose of reporting, negative impact of failure can be minimized by using a 'test when ready' approach. This is illustrated by practice in Scotland, where students are assessed by their teachers using a range of evidence from everyday activities and criteria identified in the curriculum guidelines for achievement at one of six levels. A student may be assessed as having reached a level at any time and this judgement is confirmed by moderation, either group moderation in discussion with other teachers or by using a test from an external bank of items. The test is administered individually to students who are judged to be ready for it by the teacher. In the absence of any central collection of student data, and thus of high stakes use of the results, there is no incentive artificially to inflate the numbers of pupils achieving certain levels and the results are not distorted by pressure on students. How different is this from the experience of students reported by Reay and Wiliam, who reported these observations in a Year[2] 6 classroom in England?

> In 1998 the children were working their way individually through an old science Sat paper. Fumi protested at the beginning of the session when told the children were expected to work on their own, telling the teacher, 'But we're used to working together'. Every few minutes she would sigh audibly until eventually the teacher came across to where she was sitting and proceeded to put lines through a number of Sat questions, commenting 'Don't try and do these. They'll be too difficult for you. Answer the easy ones'. Fumi struggled on for a few more minutes. It was clear to the researcher and the children sitting near her that she was crying.
>
> (Reay and Wiliam, 1999: 351)

This episode ended in Fumi rushing out of the classroom humiliated by the public airing of her supposed low ability.

There are important implications here for the school and for the wider policy context as well as for the teacher. It appears that the teacher could have explained better the purpose and expectations of the tests to Fumi. The teacher in turn would have been helped by a positive assessment culture in the school. The Assessment Reform Group has identified evidence that constructive discussion of testing and the development of desirable assessment practices in schools has a positive effect on students' self-efficacy while the exclusive focus on performance goals has a negative effect (ARG, 2002a: 6). At the national level, policy ought to avoid students being faced by tasks that are far too difficult for them and which do not allow them to show what they can do rather than what they cannot do.

## Principle 9: Assessment should be based on information of different kinds, including students' self-assessments, to inform decisions about students' learning and achievements

Curricular aims range over a number of areas or domains of learning. These are identified in different ways in the revised curricula being developed or implemented in the countries of the UK but they all include different experiences for students involving language, mathematics, scientific enquiry, physical action, artistic and musical expression, technological design and construction. Assessment that provides opportunity for students to show what they can do needs to take place in situations that elicit the different kinds of ability required in these experiences. The traditional pen and paper test fails to do this. It conveys the message to students that what is important is correctly answering certain kinds of question, with the consequence that students will judge themselves in this way, as in this further observation by Reay and Wiliam:

> For Hannah what constitutes success is correct spelling and knowing your times table. She is an accomplished writer, a gifted dancer and artist and good at problem solving yet none of those skills make her a somebody in her own eyes. Instead she constructs herself as a failure, an academic non-person, by a metonymic shift in which she comes to see herself entirely in terms of the level to which her performance in the SATs is ascribed.
> (Ray and Wiliam, 1999: 345–6)

This self-awareness could be given a far more positive role by encouraging students' self-assessment that helps their learning as well as ensuring that wider achievements are given due recognition.

Assessment within various domains should call on relevant evidence of performance in music, art, science investigations, mathematical problem-solving, and so on. But even within a domain, there are different ways of showing achievement and teacher assessment teachers is more capable of taking this into account than single format tasks or tests. In this respect there is much that can be learned from the experience of 'early years' practitioners in using the Foundation Stage Profile (QCA, 2008b). Introduced in England in 2002/3, it provides a summative assessment of children as they enter Year 1 based on wide-ranging teacher-based assessment built up over the one or two years of pre-school experience. Observations across all activities, and by all those having contact with the children, are used in making judgements about progress towards 'early learning' goals.

These judgements are reported as a profile of 13 scales relating to personal, social and emotional development, communication, language and literacy, mathematical development, knowledge and understanding of the world, physical development and creative development. It is intended that the profile is built up over the foundation stage using these various types of assessment information; the evidence is used formatively and then summarized against the performance descriptions of the scales for reporting at the end of each term. This Foundation Stage example may represent a special case but the underlying principle is that assessment information from a variety of courses will provide a richer profile of the pupil's achievements.

## Principle 10: Assessment methods should meet standards that reflect a broad consensus on quality at all levels from classroom practice to national policy

A first step in considering whether assessment is up to standard is to clarify what is meant by 'standard', a word that occurs frequently in discussions about education often with different meanings. For example, standard sometimes means the levels of performance *actually* achieved, as in referring to whether standards have risen or declined over time. Alternatively, it can mean levels of performance that it is considered *ought to be* achieved, as in the levels expected to be reached by students at certain ages. In these cases standards are taken to refer to outcomes of assessment. But there are also standards relating to the quality or properties of assessment methods, instruments and procedures used in obtaining the outcomes, one notable example being the Standards for Educational and Psychological Testing (AERA, APA and NCME, 1999).

However, none of these sets of standards captures the way in which assessment is practised and used in the classroom and the school. This book is concerned with such practice and how it can be changed to improve learning and teaching. There are no absolute standards for identifying good or improved practice, but in the process of the ARIA study a consensus emerged based on expert opinions and experience from the various assessment initiatives that were examined. It is important for these emerging standards to be made explicit so that they may be used to:

- support critical review and discussion on the nature of effective assessment in different communities of users;
- indicate the direction of progression in improving assessment practice;
- enable those developing new assessment procedures to ensure key aspects are in place.

## Standards of quality in assessment

### The meaning of standards

Two assumptions about the meaning of standards need to be clarified. The first, already mentioned, stems from confusion between standards as performance and standards as expectations. Standards are assumed to be levels of performance when, for example, they are used in referring to 'letting standards slip' or to actions taken to 'raise standards'. It means that some aspect of performance or behaviour has changed or is intended to be changed. Such standards are taken to be expectations when referring to a set of actions, a level of performance or attributes considered to be desirable. In this sense standards are a matter of judgement of what is desired and it makes no sense to talk of 'letting standards slip', since these standards are fixed expectations that are independent of actual performance.

The second assumption is that standards are expressed in terms of performance in tests or examinations. Much of the current discourse about standards concerns the achievement of students as measured by test scores or examination grades. This conception of achievement runs into difficulties in the face of the recognized deficiencies of these measurements. Earlier we noted evidence that tests and examinations fail to assess some important learning outcomes and that what they do assess is subject to unavoidable and large errors. It means that measuring the rise or fall of 'standards' by changes in scores and grades over time is flawed, since the changes are often small compared with the margins of error in the scores. In other words, we do not know whether standards, in this sense of the word, are rising or falling. Furthermore, holding teachers, schools or local authorities responsible for meeting certain standards or goals expressed as test outcomes cannot only be seen as unjust but leads to the widely recognized distortion of learning and teaching.

There remains, though, a need to know about what is happening in education and to identify whether improvement is or is not taking place. If we are to use the word 'standards' in education and avoid the deficiencies of its current conceptualization, it is necessary to dissociate the concept of standards from the implicit operational definition in terms of scores and grades. Assessment that is useful must serve the development of all important processes and outcomes of learning. When 'standards' are taken as synonymous with test scores, the whole debate about the quality of education becomes diverted into one about what is happening to test scores.

In a more general sense, 'standards' indicate levels of performance in a certain set of actions or particular values of certain attributes. Standards in the sense of decisions about expected levels of performance imply what constitutes quality in the performance or attributes. They depend in turn on decisions about what aspects of performance or behaviour are to be taken as *indicators,* the subjects of the standards. The standards describe the judgement as to what constitutes quality in relation to these indicators. Value judgements are involved in selecting the indicators as well as in deciding the levels to be expected.

For example, in assessing a student's scientific performance, the indicators used might refer to their use of inquiry skills, their application of knowledge and their communication of results. The standards describe the quality, for example, in *how* the inquiry skills are used, the application of *appropriate* knowledge and the *form* of the report. So the standards could be expressed as a description of performance, such as:

- identification of a question which can be scientifically investigated;
- application of relevant knowledge in proposing a hypothesis and making a prediction based on it;
- considered and relevant observations made and checked;
- findings used to test predictions, address the initial question and draw guarded conclusions;
- report (oral or written) presented in a logical sequence, using scientific language correctly.

Of course, this reflects a particular view of performance in science. It is conceivable that different indicators could be applied; for instance, giving preference to following instructions and getting the 'right' answer, in which case the standards would be different. So there are value judgements made about what aspects to take into account as well as about the level of performance in each. Such judgements are present in any assessment as they are involved in the choice of what to include in a test or examination.

Thus, standards are essentially qualitative descriptions that reflect value judgements as to what ought to be happening. Sadler (1989) believes they can also be expressed through examples such as the video-recording of a dance performance or the conduct of a scientific inquiry.

In education, we have national standards in the form of statements of what students ought to achieve at different stages, or levels. There are also standards that can be used in evaluation of teaching, professional development and schools (e.g., *How Good is Our School*, HMIE, 2006a). The kind of evidence required is expressed in the indicator statements; the standard expresses what quality means in relation to each indicator. Applying a standard involves a further judgement, beyond that involved in deciding the standard, about how closely the relevant evidence matches what are stated as criteria for different levels of performance. Generally, a 'best fit' approach is used, comparing the evidence with the description at the most likely level and with the levels above and below. Such judgements are an unavoidable part of assessment in education. To try to avoid them by turning the standards, and therefore the evidence, into numbers (e.g. 90 per cent at level X) leads, as is clear in current experience, to reducing the quality of education to what can be measured and counted. Moreover, the numbers convey little meaning in terms of the quality of performance.

It is, we argue, possible to conceive standards as descriptions of desired properties or performance and it is with this meaning that the word is used here.

In the projects examined in the ARIA study, which were all designed to improve assessment practice, there is in general an absence of empirical data about the effects of particular assessment reforms on students' achievements. Nevertheless, we suggest that it is feasible and acceptable to judge the value of new practices by the extent to which they meet certain standards. These standards are expressed in terms of indicators based on judgements and the principles set out above. Some are common to assessments for formative and summative purposes and some are more specific to one or the other.

Since our concern is to ensure that assessment is used to improve teaching and learning, both for the individual pupil and within the educational system, there are standards at different levels. For the individual pupil, what happens in the classroom has the greatest impact on learning; there are standards to be met if the assessment is to help learning in all the respects discussed earlier – for 'old' and 'new' basics. But what happens in the classroom is dependent on what happens at the school level in terms of assessment policy and general discourse about how assessment ought to help improve, report or measure students' achievements. In turn, school policy and practice are influenced by local authority guidance and by national policy and requirements. Hence, we can identify standards to be met by practice within each of these communities.

The standards listed below are expressed as practices to which those working in the four communities – classroom, school, local authority and national policy – should aspire.

While they are not unattainable, they express a direction rather than a goal. The notion of progression is towards the view of quality expressed by the particular standard and for this reason lower 'levels' of quality are not set out. This could be done, for example, by taking a standard such as 'Teaching provides opportunities for students to show what they can do through tasks relevant to the full range of goals of learning' and replacing 'the full range' with 'most' or 'some'. However, this would not only assume that we have evidence of the nature of progression, but would also encourage labelling of practice with 'levels' and all the problems that this entails. Rather, these standards represent the consensual views of the many expert participants in the ARIA study on what good quality looks like in a way that hopefully indicates the direction of progress for all to consider.

## Standards for classroom assessment practice

As mentioned above, the ARIA study ultimately developed quality standards for assessment for four main groups of assessment users: classroom teachers, management teams in schools, advisers and inspectors and policy makers. Through self and collective reflection as appropriate, the members of each group can use the standards in three categories as they are grouped below: the general use of assessment, its use for formative purposes and its use in arriving at summative judgements. It is possible that these standards, and the principles that underpin them, could be used as criteria for external evaluation, but their purpose is unequivocally for internal reflection and improvement whether in the classroom or in developing national policy. The aim is to encourage all stakeholders to compare their own and others' practice with the standards of good quality practice, and in doing so identify any gaps that need to be closed.

The standards for the four communities to consider are set out in Tables 2.1–2.4, in their three categories: Assessment generally, Formative use of assessment and Summative use of assessment. As will be quickly appreciated, the underlying assumption is that teacher assessment is the primary focus of the standards but ultimately it is the principle of ensuring that all assessment should assist pupils' learning that drives their formulation.

**Table 2.1** Standards for classroom assessment practice

| Assessment generally | Formative use of assessment | Summative use of assessment |
|---|---|---|
| 1. The assessment uses a range of methods that enable the various goals of learning and progression towards them to be addressed | 1. Teachers gather evidence of their students' learning through questioning, observation, discussion and study of products relevant to the learning goals | 1. Teachers base their judgements of students' learning outcomes on a range of types of activity suited to the subject matter and age of students, which might include tests or specific assessment tasks |
| 2. The methods used address the skills, knowledge or understanding being assessed without restricting the breadth of the curriculum | 2. Teachers involve students in discussing learning goals and the standards to be expected in their work | 2. Assessment of learning outcomes is based on a rich variety of tasks that enables students to show what it means to be 'good' at particular work |
| 3. Teaching provides students with opportunities to show what they can do through tasks that address the full range of goals of learning | 3. Teachers use assessment to advance students' learning by:<br>• adapting the pace, challenge and content of activities<br>• giving feedback to students about how to improve<br>• providing time for students to reflect on and assess their own work | 3. Teachers take part in discussion with each other of students' work in order to align judgements of levels or grades when these are required |
| 4. Teachers use evidence from their ongoing assessment to:<br>• help students' learning<br>• summarize learning in terms of reporting criteria<br>• reflect on and improve their teaching | 4. Students use assessment to advance their learning by:<br>• knowing and using the criteria for the standards of work they should be aiming for<br>• giving and receiving comments from their peers on the quality of their work and how to improve it<br>• reflecting on how to improve their work and taking responsibility for it | 4. Students are aware of the criteria by which their work over a period of time is judged |
| 5. Teachers develop their assessment practice through a variety of professional learning activities including reflecting on and sharing experiences with colleagues | | 5. Students are aware of the evidence used and how judgements of their learning outcomes are made |
| | | 6. Students are helped to use the results of assessment to improve their learning |

**Table 2.2** Standards for use by school management teams

| Assessment generally | Formative use of assessment | Summative use of assessment |
|---|---|---|
| 1. There is a school policy for assessment that reflects the standards in Table 2.1 for classroom practice | Teachers collaborate in developing their practice in:<br>• communicating goals and quality criteria to students<br>• helping students to take part in self- and peer-assessment<br>• providing feedback to help learning<br>• enabling students to take responsibility for their work | 1. Teachers are able to use a variety of assessment methods free from the pressure of high stakes use of the results |
| 2. The policy is regularly discussed and reviewed to reflect developing practice | | 2. Teachers take part in developing quality assurance procedures to maximize consistency in their judgements |
| 3. Teachers have opportunities to improve their assessment practice through professional learning and collaboration | | 3. Students' achievements are discussed in terms of what they can do and not only in terms of levels or grades |
| 4. Time is made available for teachers to discuss, reflect on and on occasion to observe each others' assessment practice | | 4. A manageable system for record-keeping is in operation to track and report on students' learning |
| 5. The school's policy and practice in assessment are communicated to parents and carers | | 5. Parents and carers receive written and oral reports that identify the next steps for their children and provide information about assessment processes to ensure confidence in teachers' assessment |
| | | 6. Summative judgements are required only when necessary to check and report progress |

**Table 2.3** Standards for use in national and local inspection and advice arrangements

| Assessment generally | Formative use of assessment | Summative use of assessment |
|---|---|---|
| 1. Schools' policies and practices in assessment are reviewed in relation to the standards in Tables 2.1 and 2.2 | 1. Schools' use of assessment to support learning is included as a key factor in evaluating the effectiveness of schools | 1. Schools are helped to develop action plans based on self-evaluation across a range of indicators beyond students' levels of achievement |
| 2. Inspection procedures ensure that schools evaluate their assessment practices and develop action plans for improvement | 2. Help is available for schools to ensure that all areas of achievement benefit from the formative use of assessment | 2. Advice on school assessment policies and practices takes account of what is known about the reliability and validity of different assessment methods |
| 3. There are opportunities for schools to share and develop assessment practices | 3. Schools are encouraged to develop their formative use of assessment | 3. Schools are helped to use assessment results to identify areas for improvement of learning opportunities |
| 4. Professional development is available to develop policies and improve assessment practice | | |
| 5. Resources are available to enable schools to take steps to improve assessment practice | | |

**Table 2.4** Standards for use in national policy formulation

| Assessment generally | Formative use of assessment | Summative use of assessment |
|---|---|---|
| 1. Policies require schools and local advisers to show how all assessment is being used to help students' learning | 1. Assessment to support learning is at the heart of government programmes for raising standards of achievement | 1. Moderated assessment by teachers is used to report students' performance throughout the compulsory years of school |
| 2. Introduction of new practices in assessment is accompanied by changes in teacher education and evaluation criteria necessary for their sustainability | 2. Initial teacher education and professional development courses ensure that teachers have the skills to use assessment to support learning | 2. Moderation of teachers' judgements is required to ensure common interpretation of criteria within and across schools |
| 3. Schools are accountable for using formative and summative assessment to maximize the achievement of goals | 3. School inspection frameworks give prominence to the use of assessment to support learning | 3. Regulations ensure that arrangements for the summative use of assessment are compatible with the practice of using assessment to help learning |
| 4. National standards of students' achievement are reported as a range of qualitative and quantitative data from surveys of representative samples | 4. Schools are encouraged to evaluate and develop their formative use of assessment | 4. Targets for school improvement are based on a range of indicators and are agreed through a process combining external evaluation and internal self-evaluation |

## Questions for reflection

1. Are the principles sufficiently comprehensive to cover all the main aspects of assessment in schools?

2. Choose two or three principles. What kinds of thing might be happening in different contexts if these principles were being realized in practice?

3. Are any of the standards unattainable in any particular context?

4. Choose one group of assessment users. What kinds of thing might be happening if the standards related to them were being realized in practice?

5. Is any group of stakeholders not represented by the content and aspirations of the standards? If so, how might this be addressed?

## Notes

1. Sat is the acronym for 'standardized assessment task', a name that has commonly been given to the national curriculum assessments at the end of key stages. It should not be confused with SAT, which is a registered trademark for the US-based Scholastic Aptitude Test. However, both Sat and SAT are commonly to be found in educational publications in the UK and refer to the national curriculum tasks above.

2. Primary school education in England and Wales comprises the six year groups, Year 1 to Year 6, with secondary education beginning at Year 7. In Northern Ireland children begin school at an earlier age and primary schooling runs from Year 1 to Year 7. Secondary education then begins at Year 8. In Scotland the older nomenclature of Primary 1 to Primary 7 is used (P1 to P7) with secondary schooling running from Secondary 1 to Secondary 6 (S1 to S6).

# 3   What is happening in the UK?

*Martin Montgomery*

The first chapter in this section sets out some of the major debates in assessment such as the purposes and uses of assessment, and the misapprehensions that lead to confusion over the terms 'formative' and 'summative'. The second chapter then opened up the issues of a common language, using principles and standards, for describing what we think quality in assessment practice should look like. This chapter completes the groundwork with an overview of the status and continuing developments related to teacher assessment in the four main countries of the UK.

## Introduction

Having established the language of principles and standards in relation to assessment, it is particularly interesting to review what types of change and practice are currently under way in the four main countries of the UK: England, Wales, Scotland and Northern Ireland. A review of the existing and emerging assessment systems indicates a number of trends, primary among them being the development of a more flexible approach to assessment to accommodate the following features of curriculum and pedagogy:

- greater attention to skills in teaching and learning;
- a more integrated and connected curriculum particularly in primary schools;
- a greater degree of teacher autonomy in what is taught, when and how.

As argued earlier, there has also been a distinct shift towards formative assessment with a clear move away from test-based outcomes as the sole means of measuring pupil progress and achievement. The use of sampling as opposed to wholesale testing for determining how effectively the system is working is also being considered by those who do not do it (e.g. England) and is being developed in different ways by those who do do it (e.g. Scotland).

For summative assessment, there is clearly a greater emphasis on teacher assessment in all four countries, an emphasis that in many ways recognizes both the inadequacy of testing as a means of assessing the whole curriculum and its well-documented effect of narrowing the curriculum to reflect what is and can be tested. However, in all cases this shift has generally been accompanied by a demand that whatever system is put in place, it must be robust and rigorous and must provide reliable information. The quality assurance and control measures are themselves likely causes for debate.

## What's happening in England?

England has long been seen as the citadel of testing in the UK. Tests were introduced in a rolling programme beginning with Key Stage 1 in 1991, Key Stage 2 in 1995 and in Key Stage 3 in 1993. Assessment at Key Stage 1 was made more flexible in 2005 by using teacher-assessed preset tasks and tests in various combinations depending on the expected level of attainment of the child (QCDA, 2009a). Local authorities have the statutory responsibility for the moderation of teacher assessments in Year 2 and for assessments in the highly structured Early Years Foundation Stage Profile (EYFSP) (QCA, 2008b).

At Key Stage 2, while there is teacher assessment and advice on standards, for example, how to use the Assessing Pupils' Progress (APP) (QCDA, 2009b) and other national curriculum exemplar materials, there is no formal moderation of teacher assessment beyond an exhortation for internal discussion and the building-up of portfolios of work. Key stage tests carry all the rigour and regulations of high stakes examinations. 'Optional' tests are available for all four years of Key Stage 2 leading to teacher unions' accusations of test overload (NAS/UWT, 2008). The piloting of single level tests, which can be taken twice in the school year to confirm teacher judgement, has done little to ease this perception.

Alongside this trenchant policy on testing, the Department for Children, Schools and Families (DCSF) has actively promoted its own brand of assessment for learning (AfL) in schools in England. The policy document, *The Assessment for Learning Strategy* (DCSF, 2008a) is an interesting mix of formative, periodic, summative (single level tests) and personalized learning under the AfL umbrella. While many of the principles that underpin AfL are embedded in the policy document, its framework far exceeds the 10 principles of AfL (ARG, 2002b) and its language – 'rigorously monitoring', and so on – gives the process an unexpected edge with an emphasis on summative assessment. The pilot was launched in May 2008 and offered financial incentives to those participating, a move that some have likened to payment by results.

Despite this seeming commitment to testing, and in a surprising change of policy, Ed Balls, the Secretary of State for Education in England, announced in October 2008 an end to compulsory testing at Key Stage 3 with immediate effect (DCSF, 2008b). How much the impact of the Key Stages 2 and 3 marking debacle in 2008 (*The Times*, 2008) may have hastened the decision is unknown but the 2009 marking process would certainly have been a major challenge following the termination of the contract with the US testing company, ETS. The DCSF (2009a) proposed teacher assessment based on the Assessment of Pupil Progress (APP) initiative (QCA, 2006b), as an alternative approach to the Key Stage 3 national curriculum assessments, also known as standard assessment tasks (Sats). It bundles the structured approach to periodic assessment of the APP with the development of 'Standards Files' to illustrate achievement. Support is offered to schools that take on the APP approach. They will still be able to use QCA Key Stage 3 tests but will have to do their own marking and standardizing. However the Qualifications and Curriculum Authority (QCA, 2009) has not mentioned any external moderation in the assessment arrangements for 2009.

Balls followed up on his decision to abandon national curriculum tests at Key Stage 3 by appointing an Expert Group on Assessment whose brief and parameters for action were clearly set out from the outset. It was obvious that for accountability reasons Key Stage 2 tests were here to stay. At secondary level the focus for accountability had moved away from Key Stage 3 to Key Stage 4 and qualifications, hence the relaxation in assessment and testing.

However, there was no such respite at Key Stage 2. The Expert Group, whose findings were accepted in full (DCSF, 2009b), recommended in their report (DCSF, 2009c) that there should be continued testing in English and mathematics at Key Stage 2 but testing in science should end and be replaced by teacher assessment. A more robust approach to teacher assessment at Key Stages 1 and 2 should also be developed and based on the APP initiative. They recommended the use of 'Chartered Assessors' (CIEA, 2009) and cross-key stage moderation of the Early Years Foundation Stage Profile (EYFSP), Key Stage 1 and Key Stage 2 standards. In addition, they recommended that primary and secondary schools should work together to ensure consistency of Key Stage 2 standards and that strategies for improving transition from primary to secondary schools were needed. They also proposed that there should be sample testing to monitor standards at Key Stage 3.

Interestingly, the Group did not advocate any form of moderation at Key Stage 3 as it had done for Key Stages 1 and 2. With regard to Key Stage 2, it made the following guarded statement:

> As single level tests and the Chartered Assessor models are further developed, trialled and implemented, DCSF should monitor whether a sufficiently robust moderation infrastructure exists for teacher assessment to be used as part of the accountability system.
>
> (DCSF, 2009c: 9)

Most head teacher and teacher groups; for example, the National Union of Teachers (NUT) and the National Association of Head Teachers (NAHT), support the trend towards a greater role for teacher assessment and are determined to push for a ban on testing (NUT/NAHT, 2009). However, the view is not unanimous among teachers' groups with the secondary dominated National Association of Schoolmasters/Union of Women Teachers (NAS/UWT, 2009) citing the accountability regime itself and not Sats as the root of the problem.

With the introduction of a revised curriculum at Key Stage 3 in England, and proposals out for consultation on Key Stages 1 and 2, further changes in assessment policy seem inevitable. Information that may be summarized in the 'School Report Card', which scores schools on a range of indicators; for example, attainment, pupil progress, wider outcomes, narrowing gaps, and so on can be used as a means of holding schools accountable (DCSF, 2008c).

## What's happening in Wales?

A revised school curriculum was launched in Wales in September 2008 with roll out across all year groups and key stages over the next three years. The curriculum is similar in format and process to that in the other three countries with its emphasis on the learner, skills and connected learning (see DCELLS, 2008a). It has retained a more subject-based framework than in Scotland or Northern Ireland with an emphasis on planning to deliver skills, formative assessment and connected learning, for example, through thematic teaching. The Department for Children, Education, Lifelong Learning and Skills (DCELLS, 2008b) has also required developing thinking, communication, number, information and communications technology (ICT) to be embedded in all subjects across the curriculum.

However, change was already under way; assessment policy in Wales shifted significantly following the establishment of the Welsh Assembly in 1999. Testing for 7-year-olds was terminated in 2002 and for 11- and 14-year-olds in 2005 and 2006, respectively. These changes came at a time when the value of testing was being strongly defended in England by successive education ministers. Teacher assessment supported by 'Optional Assessment Materials' replaced testing. Assessment generally has been enhanced through the use of cluster groups and extensive in-service training to support the introduction, in 2005, of the somewhat cumbersomely entitled programme: *Developing Thinking and Assessment for Learning: Development Programme* (DCELLS, 2009a), which highlights the significant overlap between thinking skills and AfL.

The policies and practice that had been developed in Wales up to 2008, endorsed by teachers (DCELLS, 2007), were subsequently used to support the revised curriculum. Having set aside testing as the principal means of judging pupil progress and achievement, the model of robust teacher assessment developed in Wales demonstrates the development of a total assessment package encompassing pedagogy, assessment process, exemplar materials and skills (DCELLS, 2008c). DCELLS (2008d) has mounted a determined attempt to promote a clear and coherent understanding of the assessment process based on internal standardization to establish standards within schools. Core and Foundation subjects in secondary schools are assessed and moderated with equal rigour: a factor that emphasizes equality of status of all subjects and not just those that are formally assessed. In addition, DCELLS (2008e) now requires primary and secondary schools to engage in cross-phase moderation through cluster groups for the core subjects – English, mathematics, science and Welsh – to establish and maintain standards.

Wales has been able to move quickly to the implementation of teacher assessment. However, certain issues remain problematic. These may work out as practice develops or may require further attention in the implementation or consolidation programmes. For example, there will be a need to ensure comparability of standards and outcomes across Foundation Phase, Key Stages 2 to 4 and beyond into the Credit and Qualifications Framework for Wales (CQFW) (HEFCW, 2009). The framework seeks to equate standards in the Foundation Stage with national curriculum outcomes and in turn with GCSE and university entry qualifications. Such comparisons are always problematic because of age and context.

There is also a major challenge in the workload associated with internal and external standard-setting and moderation particularly in the secondary sector. As stated above, Wales has opted for a total package with the support of teachers. However, maintaining the required professional levels of engagement may be more problematic, a point commented on by the NAS/UWT (2009).

The Daugherty Report (2004) had commented that schools and authorities in Wales made extensive use of non-statutory testing to supplement existing arrangements. Some tests; for example, diagnostic tests, were seen as 'compatible' but there is a persistent concern regarding overtesting. It remains to be seen to how such commercial tests will be used in Wales in the future. A key factor in this context is likely to be the role of the local education authorities and the Welsh schools' inspectorate, Estyn, in accepting teacher assessments as reliable evidence of pupil progression and performance.

## What's happening in Scotland?

Scotland has for some years actively pursued a curriculum framework that has sought to connect learning and provide a more integrated approach to teaching, learning and assessment. It has built a programme of *Curriculum for Excellence* around eight curricular areas and has developed experiences and outcomes for each. These experiences and outcomes run across six levels, effectively setting out an integrated framework for teaching, learning and assessment. The framework seeks to ensure continuity of approach from Early Years and Primary 1 (P1) to Secondary 5 and 6 (S5 and S6) in addition to the development and infusion across the curriculum of skills for learning, life and work. Great emphasis is placed upon entitlement, challenge and development of the individual learners at their own pace. However, there is concern, particularly among teachers accustomed to the more prescriptive 5–14 levels framework, that the new experiences and outcomes are too broad and do not effectively map progression. Learning and Teaching Scotland (LTScotland) is currently developing progression pathways for literacy and numeracy.

There is a well-established process of teacher assessment supported by national assessments drawn down from the National Assessment Bank (SQA, 2009a) and an apparent resistance to overassessment, a concern shared by the current Cabinet Secretary for Education and Lifelong Learning, Fiona Hyslop (Scottish Government, 2008a). At present, the sample-based Scottish Survey of Achievement (Scottish Government, 2005; LTS, 2009a) is used to monitor trends and standards in pupil achievement as opposed to the aggregation of individual data, and target-setting has been devolved to local authorities and individual schools. However, these arrangements are now under review with the introduction of Curriculum for Excellence, which will require fresh approaches to assessment.

The professional judgement of teachers is valued and parents and pupils have been extensively consulted on the proposed changes to the curriculum and on the introduction of the Assessment is for Learning Programme (LTS, 2009b). This initiative encompasses AfL, assessment of learning, assessment as learning and the use of information to move pupils, teachers and schools forward.

Since 2001, the Assessment is for Learning Programme has brought together policy makers, practitioners and researchers, supported by an ambitious programme of professional development. The positive impact of the Assessment is for Learning Programme was first documented by Condie et al. (2005). A subsequent report by Hilliam et al. (2007) targeted assessment of learning and indicated that there was greater staff inter-action and use of a wider range of teacher-led assessment strategies and sources of evidence. However, while progress was being made, they also noted that teacher assessment *of* learning was still not firmly embedded in all schools and at that stage it was still seen as work in progress.

The expectation is that the Assessment is for Learning Programme will provide a platform for teacher assessment to support the introduction of a Curriculum for Excellence. There is evidence that where local authorities have taken this approach, teachers are confident in their ability to realize the aspirations of Curriculum for Excellence (Hayward et al., 2005). As-sessment policy has still to be finalized but the Education Secretary has put down a number of significant markers for the assessment system (Scottish Government, 2009) that will support the implementation phase of Cur-riculum for Excellence. Her statements have a familiar ring and include the prerequisites that the teachers should take a leading role and their as-sessment should be rigorous and robust; pupils, parents and teachers must have reliable information about a pupil's progress, particularly in develop-ing literacy and numeracy skills; and progress and achievement should be based on clear, nationally agreed benchmarks. She also emphasized that rigorous assessment did not mean national tests.

Scotland's underperformance in the recent Trends in International Mathematics and Science Survey (Scottish Government, 2008b) has made numeracy one of the key targets for improvement. However, Black et al. (2009) recorded the interesting finding that in the consultation on the balance between teacher and external assessment for the literacy and nu-meracy qualification, a slight majority favoured a heavier weighting on external assessment than teacher assessment as it gave the qualification greater 'credibility', perhaps indicating a shift in how teachers value their own judgements or in how they are valued by others.

The Education Secretary and a local authority, Glasgow City Council, have also expressed concerns that the withdrawal of the National Assess-ment Bank, which was announced in the minister's statement (Scottish Government, 2009), could lead to an assessment/information gap (TESS,

2008). Some local authorities are piloting the use of data from teacher assessment to monitor individual school performance; for example, Angus, Edinburgh and Falkirk; other authorities; for example, Glasgow, are seeking other ways to collect data. As part of its strategy to support teacher assessment, Learning and Teaching Scotland has also recently tendered for the creation of an online 'National Assessment Resource' through which teachers, and possibly learners, can create, search for, store and print assessment resources that will match what is currently being taught. No doubt it will also be possible to incorporate additional resources to provide exemplars of the national benchmarks of progress and achievement.

## What's happening in Northern Ireland?

Northern Ireland has spent most of the last decade developing a revised curriculum and corresponding assessment arrangements for Foundation Stage and Key Stages 1 to 3, implementing them in a rolling programme since September 2007. From the outset, the Council for Curriculum, Examinations and Assessment (CCEA) has sought to marry the assessment process with curriculum and pedagogy. This has involved developing a more connected curriculum at all key stages based on 'learning areas' rather than subjects (CCEA, 2009a); a more skills-based approach to teaching, learning and assessment (CCEA, 2009b); targets for attainment in each learning area by the end of each key stage; guidelines for progression in each of the thinking skills and personal capabilities across key stages and learning areas (CCEA, 2009c); strategies for embedding AfL into classroom practice (CCEA, 2009d); and a rigorous process of teacher assessment focusing on the cross-curricular assessment of communication, using mathematics and ICT (CCEA, 2009e) to replace key stage assessment including Key Stage 3 tests in English, mathematics and science (DE, 2006).

To support the changes CCEA is proposing a series of measures. These include a new 7-level scale (CCEA, 2009f) designed to address assessment of the revised curriculum requirements and skills agenda in communication, using mathematics and using ICT across all key stages. The University of Durham's InCAS system (CCEA, 2009g) of diagnostic assessment in primary schools is to be used from Year 4 to Year 7 (the final year of primary school in Northern Ireland) to provide age-related scores for reading and general mathematics (no similar requirements were made for Key Stage 3). Extensive support is being provided for the interpretation and use of the InCAS data, including how it should be reported to parents. CCEA also provides online support for professional development and exemplar materials to illustrate standards. A standardized framework for annual reporting to parents at all key stages has also been provided, complete with exemplars (CCEA, 2009h).

The Department of Education terminated its statutory regime of Key Stage 1 and 2 assessment and statutory testing at Key Stage 3 to enable transition to the revised curriculum in 2006 (DE, 2006). However, CCEA continues to provide Key Stage 3 tests and Key Stage 1 and 2 assessment units (tasks) for schools who wish to use them. This has given rise to speculation that in the longer term a system check (assessment by sampling) may be introduced to determine if standards are being maintained.

Currently, much of the detail of the revised assessment system remains undecided. The methods of moderation and quality assurance have not been finalized and a question mark hangs over the deployment of the new 7-level scale. Indeed the Department of Education has suggested that the previous 8-level scale for English and mathematics, developed for the 1996 (DENI, 1996) version of the curriculum, should be used to assess communication and using mathematics as a way of maintaining standards (DE, 2008). However, Using ICT will be assessed using the new levels of progression.

The situation is further complicated by the rejection by grammar schools of the entrance criteria for transfer to secondary school at 11+, which have been proposed by the Education Minister, Caitriona Ruane. Grammar schools, determined to retain academic selection as their primary entry criterion, have decided to use at least two types of entrance examination. The effect of these tests on curriculum and pedagogy remains to be seen but seems likely to produce the same negative effects on teaching and learning in Years 5 to 7 as the previous Transfer Test.

All this has also to be seen in the context of the strong criticism made of the perceived failure of the literacy and numeracy strategies in schools and the assessment systems meant to support these initiatives. As success in numeracy and literacy is seen as a critical indicator of a successful education system, assessment policy in these areas is a powerful driver of the whole assessment system.

While there is general satisfaction with the revised curriculum, the situation in Northern Ireland highlights a number of key factors with regard to assessment. These include:

- the impact of external 'political' factors that limit scope for change; for example, in the transition to secondary schooling and the impact of the criticism of the numeracy and literacy strategies;
- the cultural legacy of testing; for example, at 11+ and in Key Stage 3, and the fact that CCEA and DE have to assure parents constantly that the InCAS system is not part of a new transfer procedure;

- the impact of influential groups, such as the grammar schools, in reshaping or undermining educational policy.

Despite its prolonged period of development, now almost 10 years, assessment policy and its implementation in Northern Ireland continue to be contentious, reflecting how difficult it is to break with the past and effectively match curriculum, pedagogy and assessment.

## Teacher assessment and qualifications

Regulation of examinations and vocational qualifications falls into two broad camps with England, Wales and Northern Ireland coming under the aegis of Ofqual, the Office of the Examinations and Qualifications Regulator, while in Scotland regulation is conducted through the Scottish Government advised by the National Qualifications Steering Group. With devolution each country has developed its own framework for credit and qualifications while at the same time taking cognizance of what is happening in the other countries.

### England, Wales and Northern Ireland

Ofqual, which regulates and quality controls qualifications in all three countries, is a recent spinoff from QCA, one of whose former remits was to regulate examinations and key stage assessments. For some time there had been growing concern in the area of general qualifications (GCSEs and GCEs) that coursework was open to significant abuse. The QCA (2005) report: *A Review of GCE and GCSE Coursework Arrangements* recognized the value of coursework in a range of subjects but highlighted problems of inconsistent standards, poor task setting, authenticity, recycling of work, plagiarism and Internet abuse, inconsistent moderation processes and malpractice among others. Colwill's (2007) subsequent research into how coursework could be improved led QCA to establish a framework for 'controlled assessments' for the new GCSE specifications (QCA, 2008a). These set out clear parameters for task-setting, task-taking and task-marking based on fitness for purpose and manageability. Tasks can be generated by teachers and approved and marked by the awarding body. Or they can be set and regularly refreshed by the awarding body and marked by teachers. Guidance has also been developed to authenticate coursework (QCA, 2006a).

These changes came too late to affect the launch of the revised GCE specifications but will impact on the new GCSE specifications for first teaching in September 2009. How they will work out in practice remains to be seen. Certainly, they will provide awarding bodies with greater control over coursework but one possible result is the convergence of coursework to a set of stereotypical controlled tasks that may not reflect the real teaching and learning going on in the classroom.

The timing of the revision of GCE and GCSE specifications has also meant that there has been little interaction between specification and curriculum development. In the area of skills, key skills has a significantly reduced input in GCSE and GCE specifications, yet a very high profile in curriculum development in all three countries. For this reason alone, Scotland is the most likely of the four countries to integrate its curriculum and qualifications.

In vocational areas, teacher assessment continues to have a high profile with quality assurance and control operating through accreditation and verification systems. Parity of esteem continues to be an issue. On the other hand, Wales has made a significant effort to develop 'hands-on', 'work-based learning' (DCELLS, 2009b) and incorporate achievement into the Welsh Baccalaureate to demonstrate parity of esteem and credibility.

## Scotland

Scotland has long followed its own course in national and vocational qualifications and has developed a distinct and broader approach to education at 14+ and 16+, thus deferring the early specialization characterized by the GCSE and GCE models that operate in the other three countries. Like the other countries it is developing baccalaureates (SQA, 2009b) and is promoting vocational qualifications, although in common with the other three countries parity of esteem remains an issue.

Within National Qualifications, teacher assessment is usually the sole means of assessment at levels 1–3; for example, access qualifications 1, 2 and 3. With Higher and Advanced Higher National Qualifications there are usually three teacher-assessed national units. These are supported by assessment materials that can be drawn down from Scottish Qualification Authority's National Assessment Bank (SQA, 2009a). Outcomes are moderated and exemplar materials published. A pass in each unit is a prerequisite to obtaining the final qualification but does not contribute to the final grade – that is determined by the examination alone, though the learner can appeal the final outcome.

In Black et al.'s (2009) report on the consultation *The Next Generation of National Qualifications in Scotland* respondents commented on the proposed General and Advanced general qualifications. They were marginally in favour (51 per cent) of an A–C grading for the National Units but an identical percentage did not want the units to contribute to the overall grade. Black et al. reported that 'the importance of retaining external examinations, in order to ensure consistency and credibility, was another of the more frequent comments' (p. 19, para 4.16). In Scotland, there seems to be a sense that they have got the balance right and that the higher the qualification, the greater the emphasis that should be put on external assessment.

The majority of the consultation respondents were in favour of updating qualifications in line with the Curriculum for Excellence. This is a significant challenge if transition from stage to stage is to be seamless. It will be interesting to see if the emphasis on skills and on curriculum flexibility can be carried through into the qualifications framework. The fact that Scotland has long maintained a distinct brand and approach to qualifications probably increases the chances of success. It remains to be seen where the final balance between teacher assessment and external assessment is to be struck.

In reviewing the role of teacher assessment, there is a perception, shared in all four countries, that a rigorous external examination ensures credibility especially for academic qualifications. Whether that perception takes full account of the problems of external examining and testing, pointed out by ARG (2005), is another matter.

## Conclusion

In their conclusion to the pamphlet, *The Role of Teachers in the Assessment of Learning*, ARG (2005), made the following key points:

- Robust and permanent procedures for quality assurance and quality control of teachers' judgements are needed to ensure that their summative assessment provides valid and reliable accounts of pupils' learning.
- Both pre-service and in-service professional development should extend teachers' understanding and skills of assessment for different purposes, highlight potential bias in teachers' assessment and help teachers to minimize the negative impact of assessment on pupils.
- Attention and resources must be given to creating developmental criteria, which indicate a progression in learning related to particular goals and can be applied to a range of relevant activities.
- Teachers should have access to well-designed tasks for assessing skills and understanding, which can help them to make judgements across the full range of learning goals.

- Procedures need to be transparent and judgements supported by evidence.
- Summative assessment must be in harmony with the procedures of formative assessment and should be designed to minimize the burden on teachers and pupils.

Furthermore, to avoid the negative consequences of using high stakes summative assessment to evaluate teachers and schools:

- Systems of school accountability should not rely solely, or even mainly, on the data derived from summative assessment of pupils. Such data should be reported, and interpreted, in the context of the broad set of indicators of school effectiveness.
- The monitoring of standards of pupils' achievement should be derived from a wider base of evidence than test results from individual pupils. Teachers' assessment has a place in a system in which a wide range of evidence is collected for small samples of pupils.

It is interesting to note in this review of developments in teacher assessment across the four nations just how relevant these statements continue to be. All four countries are implementing revised curricula that are more flexible and teacher/pupil-driven than those currently in place. There is a greater emphasis on skills and a determination to ensure that all learners are numerate and literate and equipped for learning, life and work. There is broad agreement that a flexible curriculum and pedagogy require a flexible system of assessment.

Taking account of the key points made above, the review of the trends in teacher assessment across the four countries has highlighted the following aspects.

### Robust and permanent procedures for quality assurance and control of teacher assessment

There is undoubtedly an emphasis on quality assurance and control through moderation. Wales has the most extensive model of moderation and, if the national curriculum tests were to be considered to have a role in moderating teacher assessment, albeit something of a stretch of the imagination, England could be argued to have the most rigorous model at Key Stage 1 and 2 but not Key Stage 3. Models for moderation in Northern Ireland and Scotland remain to be decided. However, there is concern that in the arena of high stakes qualifications the rigour and structure required for valid and reliable coursework assessment will stifle any creative approaches to assessment.

## Beginning teachers and teachers in-service

There are comprehensive policies for professional development support to promote assessment *for* and *of* learning for serving teachers but not all countries have tackled the provision for beginning teachers. In AifL in Scotland, links were built with every teacher education institution. Small grants were provided to ensure that all beginning teacher courses were informed by developments in AifL. In all four countries, websites provide a wide range of resource materials and the online delivery of in-service support is a priority for awarding bodies.

## Creation of developmental criteria

Developmental criteria are based on level descriptions but a number of countries have gone further to plot progress and achievement. For example, Wales has plotted outcomes for Foundation Stage, Scotland has already produced progression pathways for literacy and numeracy and Northern Ireland has produced progression maps for thinking skills and personal capabilities in each learning area. Most countries have provided detailed guidance/exemplar materials to demonstrate what evidence is required to make a valid judgement.

## Transparency and evidence

All four countries put a great deal of emphasis on portfolios of work to demonstrate standards. Wales and England have used online downloadable portfolios to demonstrate standards and the range of valid evidence. Northern Ireland is likely to follow. The next few years should demonstrate how effective these systems are at introducing and sustaining standards.

## Access to tasks

All four countries offer an extensive range of optional materials to support assessment. In Wales and England these tasks are frequently linked to exemplar materials, which illustrate the standards expected at particular levels. This, in effect, turns the assessment statements into artefacts that teachers can use to benchmark their own standards. The tasks can demonstrate valid evidence of achievement that goes beyond traditional text and paper-based responses. How the new controlled tasks for GCSE will work out in practice remains to be seen.

## Linking summative and formative assessment

The blending or blurring of the lines between formative and summative assessment is something at which many AfL purists might baulk, but the fact is they are two halves of the same coin. Again all four countries have sought to use one assessment process to inform the other and all recognize that the best summative assessment is one that has a strong formative dimension. The particular brand of assessment for learning adopted in England exemplifies one realization of this and has been described above as having an edge not normally associated with AfL. Any evaluation of it will make interesting reading. The concern in the context of qualifications is that high stakes assessment may drive out formative assessment.

## Broader indicators of school effectiveness

There is a move to a more value-added approach to school accountability. For example, schools in Scotland set their own targets and in Northern Ireland targets will be negotiated with the education and library board or the new Education and Skills Agency that takes over the local authority-type responsibilities in January 2010. England has consulted on a new School Report Card that has a significant value-added element.

## Sampling

Scotland already has a sampling approach to assessment through the Scottish Survey of Achievement and England is considering introducing such a system for Key Stage 3. Northern Ireland has mooted sampling as a means of monitoring standards in literacy and numeracy. However, sampling can create an assessment information gap for authorities, which they may seek to fill with commercial tests. Northern Ireland, in the absence of any 'objective' tests, has made Durham University's InCAS system a statutory part of recording and reporting to ensure a standardized approach.

## And finally

Assessment systems for 5–14-year-olds are changing in all four countries and seem to be moving towards a more teacher-led form of assessment with a strong formative emphasis. As with all pendulum swings, care needs to be taken to ensure that an appropriate, workable balance is struck in the interests of learners, teachers and the system. That said, the pendulum seems to be swinging in a different direction in high stakes qualifications.

---

## Questions for reflection

1. Consider how any two of the four countries described have attempted to deal with assessment. What common assessment issues have they faced? In what ways, if any, do their approaches differ? What compromises might be identified in each of the approaches adopted?

2. Choose one country and reflect on their practices using the standards in Chapter 2. What feedback might inform their future action?

3. What interpretation might be put on the considerable convergence of trends across the four nations? For example, does this indicate that the political investment in external assessment for accountability is finally giving way to assessment that primarily serves to support learning?

# Part II

# Spreading the word, widening the practice

# 4 What is innovative about teacher assessment?

*John Gardner*

This chapter begins the discussion about developing teacher assessment in schools. It cannot be taken as self-evident that teacher assessment is a good thing, that teachers and schools should develop their practice in this direction. There are questions to be asked about its value and whether there is credible evidence of this. Experience would suggest that the underlying philosophy of ensuring that all assessment is for the good of pupils' learning is not widely adopted, though the advances of assessment for learning (AfL) indicate a strengthening trend. Part of the challenge of increasing the integration of teacher assessment in classroom and school practices is to ensure the changes necessary are well planned from a strategic perspective. As discussed in the introductory chapter, this means that a school must address a development process involving seven processes that overlap and intertwine in a complex and progressive manner. In Chapter 1 (Figure 1.1), these were represented as: Innovation, Warrant, Dissemination, Professional Learning, Agency, Impact and Sustainable Development. This chapter considers the first two of these: what is meant by innovation in an assessment context, and what evidence gives any particular innovation a warrant that convinces teachers and others of its worth.

## Introduction

Innovation in education is a concept that defies simple definition, dependent as it is on the context in which it arises and the wide variety of social dimensions that the change process involves. Early work on educational innovation tended to focus on curriculum reform, such as the ground-breaking developments of the Schools Council/Nuffield Humanities Curriculum Project (1969–1972), or on theories of the 'innovation decision' process as derived from the empirical work of Rogers (1962) on aspects of the US agricultural industry. Much of what was written then and since centred on the transformation from concept or idea to policy and practice. As a consequence, the education literature is not short of evaluations of the innovations, including a modest corpus relating to assessment, that have swept through the system in the last 20–30 years. This chapter looks specifically at the concept of innovation in assessment but acknowledges that it is rarely easy to concentrate exclusively on an innovative idea without consideration of processes such as dissemination, which is dealt with in Chapter 5. This process and its allied professional learning activities sponsor the sharing of ideas and experimentation and the perspectives of those who are newly engaged begin to modify the original ideas and practices as they make their own contribution. As Schön (1971) observed '... innovation does not by any means entirely antedate the diffusion process; it evolves significantly within that process' (p. 107).

Innovation, even with high intrinsic value, may be of little interest if there is no attempt to transform it to routine practice, where 'routine' is not merely automatic but signifies that it is sufficiently well regarded and used, and it constitutes commonly expected practice. However, existing practice cannot be transformed unless an appropriate innovation is brought to the fore. Consequently, this chapter focuses on the concept of innovation itself, while reflecting at some points on the processes that bring it to wider audiences and application, and ultimately to sustained implementation.

## The nature of innovation

Sometimes in scientific or medical contexts, innovation may be almost serendipitous, arising from chance and good fortune. More often than not, however, it will be the result of years of painstaking research; for example, in some genetics contexts. In education, innovation is not as likely to be a discrete outcome of a research process or even a '... tidy picture of a coolly managed process' as Rudduck (1976: 5) prefaced her report on the humanities project. Conceding that the report may have been misleading in this respect, she acknowledged that it missed the '... puzzlement and opportunism that characterize such ventures ... and the sense of responding to events rather than controlling them'; a picture more resonant of innovation by evolution than revolution, however dramatic the ultimate shifts in practice may appear to be.

Arguably, therefore, educational innovation emerges in a more 'organic' fashion. For example, it may follow a bottom-up variant of Rogers's centre-periphery model in which a new idea emerges at the researcher/ teacher interface, captures the interest of increasing numbers of teachers and grows from its small beginnings to eventual adoption by whole sectors of education. AfL and its espousal in the UK was just such an innovation that grew from the seminal review of research on formative assessment by Black and Wiliam (1998a) and from a subsequent, enthusiastic uptake of the key findings by teachers and schools. By way of contrast, the history of using computers in the classroom has been considerably more problematic. The introduction of computers has closely followed the top-down centre (government) to periphery (school) variant of Rogers's classical model, but has arguably not been effective in promoting classroom transformation despite the massive 'seeding' afforded it in successive waves of multi-million pound funding initiatives by government. As a major educational policy innovation, largely isolated from the operational context of schools, it is debatable whether it is viewed more as an end in itself than a means to improving learning. To all accounts this particular innovation continues to stutter. For example, the Office for Standards in Education (OFSTED, 2004) has reported that '... the government's aim for ICT to become embedded in the work of schools [is] a reality in only a small minority of schools ...' despite '... good evidence to suggest that most teachers regard ICT positively, with only a residual minority of the profession reluctant to take their work forward with ICT' (p. 6). Despite teachers accepting the use of computers in education as a 'good' thing, it has not been enough to initiate the deeper changes necessary for integrating it into practice, a phenomenon also identified by James and Pedder (2006) in AfL contexts.

The last few decades in education have also seen the rise of the gurus or evangelistic educationalists who purvey ideas and innovations with a charismatic panache. They take large numbers of their audience through the first two 'knowledge' and 'persuasion' stages of Rogers's (1983) five-stage innovation-decision process ('decision, implementation and confirmation' being the subsequent stages, p. 20). Thinking skills, multiple intelligences and AfL are all recent examples of inherently important educational innovations in educational practice or theory. However, they have also become vulnerable to criticism from traditionalists, primarily because they have been the subject of relatively trivial expositions by some 'true believers'. Replete with classroom anecdotes, the appeal of the guru's message to hard-pressed teachers is often sufficiently seductive for them to launch straight into a regime of tips and tricks. However, the effect can be very short-lived as the same teachers soon jettison them because the cycle of reflection and action has not been fully engaged and the deeper theoretical and philosophical assimilation of the innovation has been missed. As Fullan (1993) puts it: 'It is not enough to be exposed to new ideas. We have to know where new ideas fit, and we have to become skilled in them, not just like them' (p. 16).

The increased importance of reflection for promoting improvement and innovation in all forms of successful professional practice is usually attributed to the work of Schön (1983). Although his examples are largely drawn from industry, they recount a symbiotic relationship, mediated by reflection, between theory on the one hand and empirical knowledge on the other. His outline of the invention of the junction transistor at Bell Labs (p. 181) charts a process in which '. . . reflection on theory leads to experiment . . . [then] . . . reflection on the unexpected results of experiment leads to theory, or to invention'. Shockley, the principal scientist involved in this example, reputedly called this method 'creative failure methodology' (compare this with Schön's euphemistic 'unexpected results') but the essence of it was the experimentation and reflection on the results. When teachers try out new (to them) techniques, the hope is that they will also reflect on 'what works', thereby using their own experience to amend any accompanying theory that has been designed to explain the proposed effectiveness or application of the techniques. And just like Shockley's experience, any innovation or invention in classroom assessment may be prone to initial 'failure' and reflective revision, sometimes humorously summed up as the 'Ready! Fire! Aim!' cycle.

Innovation in assessment, then, is often promoted at the level of the individual by encouraging the trialling of new methods, evaluating their effectiveness and worth, and modifying practice in the light of this reflection. The notion rarely holds that the worth of an innovation is self-evident or guaranteed by theory; implementation or trialling at some level is a clear requirement. Innovation in assessment needs sufficient visibility for the individual to be aware of it, know how it operates and what can be achieved. Ultimately teachers need to experiment with the innovation in order for them to begin to transform their own practice.

## Innovation in assessment

In science and medicine, major innovations are often definably 'new' and discrete (e.g. a new drug) while in education they can be reincarnations of older practices, or new ways of carrying out established activities, all cast as innovative. What, then, do we understand innovation in assessment to be? The dictionary definition might lead us to expect a 'new' type of assessment, new in terms of the methods used or the process undertaken, or indeed the focus. The much quoted 'new learning' heralded by twenty-first-century technology and its impact on society arguably presents significant assessment challenges, the resolution of which may well constitute innovation. There are various candidates for this new learning. For example, QCA (2007a) launched a framework for learning and thinking skills.

This covers the need for learning and, by implication, assessment in areas such as: teamworking, independent enquiry, self-management, reflective learning, effective participation and creative thinking. An input by Baker (2007), the then President of the American Educational Research Association (AERA) has also heralded the need to assess adaptive problem-solving, risk assessment, managing distraction, self-management and changeable roles.

As a new focus for learning, any approach to appraising skills of 'distraction management' might, therefore, have a legitimate claim to being innovative. More often than not, however, the newness identified in innovative contexts is in fact 'situated' or context-dependent. In most situations, it is probably fair to say that the assessment process is not so much new *per se* as it is new to those people, those circumstances, those places, and so on.

Take for example formative assessment, assessment that is designed to support learning. The importance of this form of pedagogically integrated assessment has come to the fore in recent years. Based primarily on Black and Wiliam's (1998a) review of the research evidence supporting the effectiveness of formative assessment in promoting learning, ARG (2002b) launched its 10 principles to promote and guide the practice of AfL. AfL has been a force for change in classroom practice in national assessment systems in the four nations of the UK (see Chapter 3) and wider afield in, for example, the USA, Canada and Europe (OECD, 2005). It could therefore be perceived in some quarters as an assessment innovation that has swept across the global education landscape, fulfilling one of Mayer's (1991) indicators of successful innovation: the transfer of 'content, methods and actions...the creation of connections between "different disciplines...different teachers, their methods, their value systems and their behaviours"' (cited by Elliott, 1993: 60). A more grounded view might be that it merely constitutes good pedagogical practice being introduced in places in which more didactic practices had long held sway. Such 'places' might be as singular as a teacher's classroom or as cross-cutting as all schools in a particular local authority. They certainly include whole sectors such as higher education, where a sea-change in assessment approaches over the last decade has fostered such 'new to the sector' innovations as peer- and self-assessment, and criteria sharing (see, for example, Boud and Falchikov, 2007 and Bryan and Clegg, 2006).

Identifying innovation, therefore, is not a simple matter of perceiving a change that some consider to be novel. As this argument would imply, we must first identify whether it is widely recognized as genuinely novel and perhaps even experimental, never having been used before or used only in very localized and isolated circumstances. If this test fails, we must next determine if it is contextually new: new to primary classrooms in general, to a set of schools (such as a local authority), to a specific school or indeed to a particular group of staff or individual teachers.

Simply registering a change of practice as 'innovative', and then attempting to appeal to a person's curiosity and professional interest, can be damaging. Indeed, such an approach may well constrain further development if those who are the targets for adopting the innovation do not recognize its novelty aspect or, worse, see through and reject it, perceiving instead a top-down directive that is designed to promote some form of unilateral behaviour change. From another perspective, however, using words like 'innovation' can serve as the Trojan horse that avoids telling the target group that their current practice is inadequate!

Effective adoption of an innovation is widely considered to be dependent on its 'ownership' by those who must adopt it; ownership being more to do with personal beliefs, and the promise of self-benefit and benefit for their students, than mere changes in practice or behaviour. As Morrish (1976) put it: 'People generally accept innovations more readily if they understand them, regard them as relevant to their particular situation and also help to plan them' (p. 129).

## Types of innovation in assessment

Given the caveats above, it is something of a tall order to identify the types of innovation that may be encountered in assessment contexts. Broadly speaking, they form a gradation in 'newness'. Beginning with arguably the least innovative and ending with the most, let us call these:

- innovations in administration (facilitating assessment processes, record-keeping and reporting);
- situated innovation (assessment practice that is new in the circumstances);
- innovations for 'new learning' (new aspects of assessment specifically addressing twenty-first-century goals).

### Innovations in administration

Perhaps among the easiest 'innovations' to identify are those that relate to the administrative processes of assessment. Assessment carried out through the medium of computers, for example, is often misleadingly described as an innovation in assessment when it is more precisely viewed as an innovation in the administration of the assessment. Computer-based or online offerings stretch the concept of innovativeness if they are merely pen-and-paper tests presented on screen, with the examinee's responses typed directly into the system. There certainly was a time when assessment through the medium of a machine was a new and frontier-pushing development (e.g. with Pressey's 1926 'simple apparatus that gives tests and scores') but the assessment *per se* was no different from that which could be carried out by a person; it was simply considered more efficient.

This is still the case today. The potential for cost savings and administrative efficiencies are aspects of standard online assessments that are regularly argued as selling points. However, they fail any reasonable test of innovativeness in assessment itself. Objectivity is another selling point but even here the concept is made manifest in a relatively minor way. The claimed objectivity may be based on applying indisputably correct answers in a process that could be carried out just as objectively by human judges (a simple example of the type of item might be the case of 4 being the indisputable answer to $2 + 2 = ?$). Or it might be based on the application of fixed answers, previously interpreted and supplied by human judges and therefore potentially subject to the human error they purport to defend against. It is therefore not quite the holy grail-like objectivity of no human error. Nor is it the 'objectivity' of finely honed subjective judgements that have been reviewed and endorsed by several to many human judges in a rigorous moderation process.

A significant step up from the test that is merely computer-based is what is known as an adaptive test, headlined by the in-vogue computerized adaptive tests (CATs) of recent years. In the case of CATs there is perhaps more justification to apply the term 'innovation in assessment'. Adaptive testing is a relatively dynamic form of assessment that proceeds in a cycle. The first assessment of the pupil identifies the level of difficulty in terms of items that they can manage. The next stage of the examination process is then tailored to a level of difficulty at and above the assessed capability level. Again, the level of difficulty the pupil can manage is reassessed. The test continues through these cycles of tailored assessment until the pupil can no longer 'master' the level of difficulty of the examination questions being presented.

In a paper version, the process would be very limited and self-directed; for example, 'If you have answered questions 5 to 7 correctly, please proceed to Section D, Question 11 ...', and so on. The considerable perseverance and honesty required of anyone taking a paper-based 'programmed' learning test rules it out in most cases but the computerized versions are considered to carry out assessment and capability levelling processes, such as attributing pupils' work to national curriculum levels more rapidly and objectively. The innovation lies in the development of sophisticated algorithms for calibrating a large collection of assessment items, establishing the level of difficulty at which a pupil is currently working and processing their pathway through the items at appropriately increasing levels of difficulty. The conclusion that proponents of CATs promote is that the last level the pupil can manage is an accurate measure of their achievement. Simple as it might sound, systems based on this approach have significant failings (see, for example, Way et al., 2006 and Wise and Kingsbury, 2000) but over time many of these are responding to increasing refinement and sophistication. Various claims are made about their ability to deal with more complex assessment contexts such as those presented by the creative and expressive learning domains (see, for example, Embretson, 2003) but in most existing cases CATs are best suited to multiple-choice and fixed answer designs.

## Situated innovation

Part of the argument under this heading hints at a restricted type of innovation in assessment; namely, that which is new in the circumstances in which it is introduced or observed. Consider a classroom in which a history teacher reads from a chosen specialist text on an aspect of history that the students must study. The students listen and eventually the teacher closes with 'Any questions?', possibly in that perfunctory manner which signals that questions are not really expected or desired. The essay assignment is given; the end of class is signalled. A bit 1950-ish perhaps, but this type of learning experience is not exactly extinct. Clearly, it would be an innovation if, in another scenario, such a teacher engaged the students more directly, in debates, role plays, site visits, research tasks, project work, and so on or even more simply in genuine one-to-one, group or whole class discourse about the matters under study. Such pedagogical tools are known to be effective in promoting deeper learning and would be innovative in the circumstances of the classroom described. However, arguably, it would be a further innovative step if the teacher were also to integrate assessment formatively into the learning process through appropriate sharing of learning objectives and success criteria, questioning, feedback, self- and peer-assessment, and the identification of next steps to improve the assimilation of the learning.

The two 'improved' scenarios above could be described as arising from innovation in the teacher's approach; the one more specifically pedagogical; the other relating to the use of assessment to support learning. However, experience has shown (e.g. James et al., 2006a; Leitch et al., 2006) that in some classrooms these 'innovations' may not be deeply assimilated into professional practice. Instead, they may be treated superficially as a set of teaching tips for improving student engagement and motivation to learn; innovative in the circumstances but not reaching the potential for which they are designed. As Fullan (1993: 23) comments: 'It is no denial of the potential worth of particular innovations to observe that unless deeper changes in thinking and skills occur there will be limited impact'. Arguably, of course, any means to improve students' engagement and motivation, however limited, are surely to be welcomed.

Whether treated superficially or deeply espoused, it is clear that formative techniques would not be considered innovative in circumstances in which teachers have an underpinning grasp of the importance of using assessment to support learning and already use some or all of them in their day-to-day practice.

Knowing when something is innovative with good, long-term impact and not merely a novelty that promotes short-term success, is not a widely held skill. For this reason, the need for a deep understanding of what may be a purposeful innovation cannot be underplayed. Too often teachers, the school system and policy makers are regaled with the latest ideas. Some of these are not much more than fads but have been cast in the 'must do' urgency of some of the less thoughtful voices in the school improvement lobby or indeed from policy makers with short-term political agendas.

Arguably, at the root of all calls for change today is the aspiration to improve the learning experience and outcomes for every student in every classroom, through the improved teaching and facilitation of learning by their teachers. The continuous cry of falling standards reverberates through the system whether aimed at national examinations (GCSEs, A-levels, etc.) or at basic skills (levels of literacy and numeracy, etc.). Yet many commentators and researchers reject the notion that the standards in use in education in England, for example, have other than a very limited value in appraising the quality of education. One of these commentators, Mansell (2007), contends that any mention of standards should come with a 'health warning' (p. 26). In his view, the public notion that *raising standards* means raising the quality of the education provided is seriously out of kilter with the reality in schools, and that the concept of *raising standards* is reified in many schools simply in the aim to raise test scores.

This phenomenon of the link between standards and examination outcomes continues despite the many deep-lying social issues that are known to mingle with the educational and pedagogical dimensions of schooling. Inevitably, it is schools that take the brunt of both the blame and the responsibility for rectifying what is in essence a misconceived issue. And the ensuing calls for change command an audience at the highest levels from government departments through their statutory curriculum and assessment agencies to local authorities. Action, often cloaked in the terminology of innovation, typically plays out through government consultations, pilot studies, professional development programmes and voluminous resources, often online, on CD/DVD disks or in glossy printed packages. None of these actions warrants criticism *per se* but they have the potential to suggest a patronizing 'we know what is best and what you should do' approach that seems to have missed the decades of ineffective impact on which those proposing such an approach could reflect. However, this is not to say that it is unnecessary to have good resources or evidence from well carried out pilot studies; who would not benefit from having them when undertaking an innovative change to their practice?

### Innovations for 'new learning'

'New learning' is a term that is bandied around the education system, nationally and internationally, with only the most basic of commonly held understandings and no widely accepted definition. As more or less a sound-bite concept, it can attract an audience with policy makers, academics and teachers alike, much quicker than most educational issues. But it is likely that these various audiences hear different things. The 'knowledge that is of most worth' in today's society could arguably draw on Herbert Spencer's 'science', a continuously evolving adaptation to the modern world, probably more generally couched in terms of 'new' skills that are perceived as necessary. To policy makers it might be literacy, numeracy and ICT skills; to society more generally it may be aspects of citizenship, and to academics it might be thinking skills or skills to manage distraction. Whether the target knowledge, understanding or skill is actually new or simply in vogue, the question arises as to what form of assessment best addresses it.

Much of what is claimed to be innovative in assessment actually derives from considerations of how validity in the making of assessment judgements may be improved. For several decades there has been a rumbling unhappiness with psychometric and standardized testing programmes, the types of assessment that give rise to scores, marks and grades. The reputed high reliability and acknowledged high costs of external testing have also come under significant fire in the UK; the former because it is not always the case; the latter because it is largely unwarranted (for a brief summary of the positions on reliability and cost, see Gardner 2007). Such measures have little meaning in relation to the learning they have been used to assess and generally have even less prospect of contributing formatively to students' learning. The consequences of their dominance, however, include 'wash-back' damage on other aspects of the system:

> ... increasing the use of externalized methods and reporting [it] has eroded trust in the professional judgement of education practitioners to deliver assessment in other contexts. Above all, it has had increasingly serious consequences for the system's overall fitness for purpose.
>
> (Skidmore, 2003: 45).

A variety of alternative or innovative methods of assessment have flourished over the same several decades, as a means of raising the ante on validity. All of them have relatively shaky histories in terms of adoption, owing partly to the continued hostility of some influential policy makers towards anything perceived as subjective assessments and partly to the logistics and costs of the moderation and validation of the judgements provided. The overarching innovations in question can be conveniently classified as coursework and authentic assessment.

Coursework covers a number of possible assessment vehicles, including portfolios, project work, exhibitions and oral presentations. It has had a chequered history and indeed has often suffered a lack of confidence (and therefore investment) in the teacher assessments used, the standards of work achieved or the fear (with some justification) of significant plagiarism or third-party support for any of the unsupervised aspects of the work. Recent moves in national examinations at GCSE level in England, Wales and Northern Ireland (QCA, 2008a) have witnessed the introduction of 'controlled assessment', which may address some of the perceived problems (see Chapter 3 for further information on controlled assessment).

The early 1990s also saw the emergence of the concept of 'authentic assessment', particularly in the USA. Initially promoted as a high-validity alternative to the perceived low validity of external and state or national testing, it aims to assess learning in a manner that relates more closely to the way in which the learning content arises from or affects students' daily lives. Authentic assessment therefore avoids psychometric or externally administered tests, using instead the same types of assessment approaches as are used in coursework; for example, portfolios, research-based projects, presentations and exhibitions. However, even the 'everyday life' innovation of authentic assessment seems to have lost its way in some quarters where it now exists primarily as a 'rubric-based' approach to integrating curriculum, performance standards and assessment.

A rubric, as the name suggests, prescribes the type of learning to be undertaken, the assessment criteria to be used and the standards of performance onto which the criteria map. Widely used in the USA, the example of Performance Standard 24B.E (Illinois 2007) illustrates the model. This health education rubric requires teachers to develop students' competence in applying their knowledge and exercising their decision-making skills in two out of four 'real' life scenarios provided. These paragraph scenarios describe an incident and the rubric identifies how the students' responses to a prescribed decision-making process should be graded. Electronically scanned examples of student work that either 'meet' or 'exceed' the standards of performance are also provided to complete the all-encompassing nature of the rubric guidance. Assessment by teachers may be an innovative element of this approach but the dependence on pre-ordained rubrics arguably gives an up-to-date meaning to Dewey's (1938) counsel that: 'Nothing has brought pedagogical theory into greater disrepute than the belief that is identified with handing out to teachers recipes and models to be followed in teaching' (p. 170).

A major element of the debate about assessing new learning, though not always acknowledged or expressed, is that a focus on content is potentially no longer valid. If a curriculum aspires to develop autonomy or self-reflection, one question for the assessment community might be: Can these be assessed without recourse to content-based proxies? How valid is the assessment made of a student's 'ability to work as a member of a team' when it is based on a process that attempts to disaggregate the individual contribution from that of collective endeavour in a group project? At essence, the central question arising in relation to assessing new learning might be conceived as: Is this judgement of what a person knows/has learned/understands and so on, valid in terms of the evidence used to make it and the process used to collect the evidence?

Green (1998) counsels us to remember that 'judgement' has at least two meanings. In an assessment context, the first would be the process of assessing and deciding the level of achievement and quality of a student's work and the second would be the category decision itself (i.e. a grade, level or score). He argues that such judgements are never merely subjective (e.g. whimsical or unsupported by evidence) as they are always based on '. . . reasons, grounds, rules or principles' (p. 178) or, as might otherwise be argued, on the evidence available against commonly held standards and level descriptions. However, it is entirely possible, and not uncommon, for two assessors to interpret the same evidence and arrive at a different judgement or for two assessors to examine different types of evidence and arrive at different judgements about the same performance. In the complex scenarios of new learning, such challenges are writ large.

Innovative types of evidence or means for collating it, which are designed to increase the validity of evidence on which assessments are to be made, are only part of the story. Take, for example, the humble UK driving test. Not so long ago the 'knowledge' part of the test was carried out through Highway Code questions, which were randomly chosen by the examiner and presented orally at the end of the practical driving test. The aspiring driver could be 'failed' for answering a question incorrectly, even if the practical aspects had been exemplary. More recently the examination involves a computer-delivered 'knowledge' test, the passing of which, at a preset threshold, determines whether the student driver proceeds to the practical test. This test enables their competence in practical driving skills to be assessed, with the examiner's assessments largely governed by preordained competence thresholds. However, the examiner retains a degree of discretion over elements relating to the student's control of the vehicle, smooth use of gears and brakes, and so on. What then might constitute innovation in this assessment setting?

Validity is clearly an issue. Yes, the computer-based test is an efficient, cost-effective and objective means of testing certain types of knowledge relating to driving. And, yes, the practical test is a relatively valid means of accessing actual competence. But it is a test of only 50–60 minutes' duration, which cannot cover all possible driving situations, manoeuvres and skills. In assessment terminology, the validity of this test, in common with the large majority of tests in any context, is challenged by the restricted learning domain that it is able to assess in the time and circumstances. What might be innovative in this context, therefore, would be the keeping of a log of the driving experiences as the student driver is learning how to drive. This could serve as evidence for accredited instructors to vouch for the competence of their student drivers, when they judge it appropriate. The analogy could extend to the obvious challenges such a 'more valid' system might present, but there is general wariness about the dependability of tutors' judgements of their own students' performance in many contexts, not least when the judges are teachers in schools. However, if these judgements are made in constrained circumstances for the various types of 'new' learning under scrutiny, all the existing challenges to validity (and reliability) will likely persist and become even more vulnerable to negative critical scrutiny.

## Conclusion

Since the 1960s and 1970s, the psychometric grip of the psychologists on assessment in schools (and elsewhere in education) has been progressively challenged in relation to the unwarranted claims of reliability in many instances and to a lack of validity in most. In parallel with these challenges, there has been a rising demand for meaningful assessments, which in turn has given rise to a plethora of innovative approaches to assessment, variously hailed as authentic, valid and purposeful. Today, alternative and 'innovative' approaches to assessment in schools include portfolios, project work and presentations. But such innovations in assessment may not be all that they seem; indeed, they may not be innovations at all.

Central to all of them is the practice of assessment and judgement-making by teachers, for both summative and formative purposes. What has been argued in this chapter is that in many respects, the innovative dimension of some approaches may not actually be an innovation in assessment; it may be more of an innovation in assessment administration or a situated assessment innovation that is 'new' to the teacher, to the school or to the circumstances in which it is introduced. Alternatively, it may be innovative in assessment, in, for example, striving to address important and currently unfulfilled assessment needs, such as those demanded by the curricular and pedagogical pursuits of 'new learning'. It is important therefore to analyse an innovation to determine whether it is actually innovative and, if so, in what circumstances and why it is considered innovative. Once determined, these will contribute to a better understanding of what is being proposed as an innovative change in educational practice. This will in turn contribute to considering how effective it has been, what value it may hold for the target audience and how best it may be transformed into well-regarded and common practice.

## Questions for reflection

1. What would be the features that would identify a certain practice of teacher assessment as an innovation rather than a part of regular practice?

2. What information and experiences with an innovation in teacher assessment would be required to prompt others to integrate it into their practice?

3. How might innovations be introduced and developed to promote changes in both understanding and practice?

4. Reflect on a recent assessment innovation. To what extent was this introduced and developed in ways consistent with ideas in this chapter?

# 5 Moving beyond the classroom

*Louise Hayward*

This chapter considers another important facet, dissemination, of the process of developing teacher assessment as a major change in schools. It explores why growing ideas beyond classrooms so often feels like pushing boulders uphill. It begins by looking at different models of dissemination that have been developed in practice by those trying to extend policies and change practices across schools, local authorities and indeed national systems. Examples are used to illustrate differences between dissemination to transmit and transform ideas and practices. Consideration is also given to 'what matters?' if ideas and practices are to be disseminated in ways that will influence policy and practice.

## Introduction

The idea of improving education by the growth of ideas and changing practices, beyond individual teachers to the wider school or indeed local and national systems, has been a troubling one over time and across educational communities. Projects that are successful in their early stages with individual teachers often fail to be sustained on a broader scale. They either fail to grow beyond individual classrooms or fail to engage schools beyond those originally involved in the development of the ideas and practices. The idea of dissemination is common in the discourse of research, policy and practice but exactly what it means is less clear. If the implication of dissemination is that ideas and practices are grown within and across schools, then the concept of dissemination has had a difficult past. It also has a complex present and may have an uncertain future. Cuban's (1994) analysis of the relationship between innovation and change suggests that, whatever the intentions of research or policy communities, the impact on practice may be limited: 'Hurricane winds sweep across the sea tossing up twenty foot waves; a fathom below the surface turbulent waters swirl while on the ocean floor there is unruffled calm' (p. 2).

Fullan argues that even when policy initiatives have been perceived to have had some influence, the 'top-down' and 'bottom-up' models of dissemination in common practice never achieve more than partial success.

> . . . even the most sophisticated centrally-driven reform – what has come to be called 'informed prescription' – can only take us part way toward the solution; on the other hand, even highly supported decentralized strategies which seek 'a thousand flowers to bloom' do not take us very far (not enough flowers bloom; good flowers do not get around or amount to critical mass breakthroughs).
>
> (Fullan, 2004: 6)

This is arguably true whether it is a head teacher or a government agency promoting the new practices through informal prescription.

### Models of dissemination

Two major approaches to dissemination have been common in recent years; one based on ideas of transmission and a second based on ideas of transformation. The first of these, dissemination as transmission, is very much the traditional approach and is considered next.

## Dissemination as transmission

In common usage, dissemination is defined as 'to scatter or to spread abroad'. In education, the term is commonly used with the implication of intentionality, where there is an intention that the ideas and practices will become familiar to increasing numbers of teachers and schools. There have been several different approaches to dissemination as transmission of ideas, a selection of which are discussed here. All these approaches have a common theme; they are based on the idea that change happens through the dissemination of information.

### The scattergun model

> By disseminating examples of good practice, practical hints and tips for using ICT, news of recent developments, information about new ideas and details of professional development opportunities in this field, the magazine enables readers to apply this knowledge in their everyday practice.
>
> (Connected, 2006)

This example of an innovation in ICT illustrates a scattergun approach to dissemination, where numerous possibilities are offered to teachers to use as they see fit. The term 'scattergun' might seem pejorative if we were to interpret the list of ideas contained in the cited example as random. However, it is possible that the authors intended that a range of approaches to the dissemination of ideas should be offered; recognizing that any single approach was unlikely to be effective with all teachers. Most commonly the target of this approach is teachers in schools. It is less commonly used in disseminating educational ideas across policy or research communities. One potential advantage of such an approach is that it offers choice to those involved in the process of change.

## Resource-based models

A common approach to the dissemination of ideas has been to develop resources that are offered to schools or local authorities using a number of strategies.

The *saturation strategy* involves sending copies of a particular resource to every school and in some cases to every teacher. This has been used most commonly with policy documents; for example, in Scotland the 5–14 Curriculum and Assessment documents were distributed in this way. In some cases resources are supported by staff development. Taking the Assessment 5–14 policy in Scotland (SOED, 1991) as a case study, a folder of staff development activities was developed to support teachers developing their understandings of and practices in the policy document. However, the dissemination for the staff development activities was different. These were distributed to local authorities who had the option of issuing them to schools or using them as part of staff development events.

The *selective dissemination strategy* involves a more limited model of issuing resources. Here, resources are targeted towards individuals who are perceived to have an interest in, for example, assessment, and are invited to act as an advocate for the ideas within their own community of interest.

A potential advantage of this approach is that it offers the opportunity for resources to support development being available in individual schools or classrooms. However, there is a history of resources in schools, classrooms or in local authorities collecting dust rather than having any impact on practice. This problem has remained even when resources have been mediated by staff development events. A further disadvantage is that teachers and schools have at times been overwhelmed by the number of resource packs coming into schools. In Scotland, the *self-selecting strategy* emerged at least in part as a reaction to schools' perceptions that they were drowning in paper. A policy decision was taken to develop resources, advertise them and invite schools to request any that were of interest to them. It was intended that the selection of resources would link closely to priorities within each school's development plan. One advantage of this approach was that it gave control over the introduction of ideas to schools themselves, most commonly to head teachers. However, it also led to a rather haphazard link between schools and resources, with schools often being unaware of what might be available to support their own priorities.

A further resource-related dissemination strategy has had rather more success than some of the models outlined earlier, the *marketing programme strategy*. Approaches to learning and teaching in reading and mathematics are often governed by teachers' use of commercial programmes that provide graded activities for learners. The graded activities claim to offer clear progression and many primary schools use programmes from publishers such as Heinemann, Ginn, Oxford Reading Tree and Longmans. This strategy is interesting in that it has not been initiated by policy makers or local authorities, among whom there may be mixed views. Some members of the policy community would argue that publishers' programmes help ensure a reasonable experience for all learners. Others argue that these programmes interfere with or even substitute for teachers' thinking about children's learning and are, therefore, not to be encouraged. It is interesting to speculate on the reasons why this model of dissemination has been so powerful. The publishers have significant advertising and marketing budgets that no doubt exert an influence, but there are likely to be other factors involved. The resources are comprehensive and can be used throughout the school. They often advertise their link with educational theories and in many cases are supported by staff development. Undoubtedly, a further factor is the manner in which schools can become 'locked' into a specific scheme because of their cost. Once a school has made a decision to adopt a particular resource, it is a very expensive business to change that decision.

The commitment to detailed, sometimes fairly restrictive resources, tends to imply that teachers depend on them because of their own fairly low-skill base in the area. The resources are considered able to compensate for the deficit by providing resources that would assure a certain level of educational opportunity is made available to each learner. The detailed tasks and teachers' notes provide very detailed training to lead teachers through complex ideas. In some ways developments in the early phases of the literacy strategy in England were consistent with this approach.

The examples offered until now have largely been based on the dissemination of ideas from what have been assumed to be relatively more powerful groups; for example, policy makers, researchers or publishers, to what have been assumed to be relatively less powerful groups; for example, teachers and schools. More recently, another model of dissemination of ideas across communities has become increasingly common. The *sharing good practice strategy* involves the identification of ideas in practice, most often in schools or within classrooms, followed by the wider dissemination of these ideas across wider groups. Most commonly, practice that is perceived to be good is identified in schools and in classrooms by more powerful groups; for example, policy makers, school inspectors or researchers and then promoted or shared across the mainly practice communities. Examples are offered of how ideas have been made real in classrooms. More sophisticated models of this approach encourage practitioners to tell their own stories of practice and to make explicit the process of change, identifying problems faced and issues addressed. The idea of sharing practice as an important part of improving schools is presently a powerful one. For example, in Improving Scotland's Schools (HMIE, 2006b), the 'state of the nation' report on education, based on evidence from school inspections during 2002/5, there are 20 references in the text to 'good practice'. There are three references to good practice as something identified by Her Majesty's Inspectorate of Education (HMIE), five to sharing good practice as an area for development, three to sharing good practice as a strategy for improvement and nine references to sharing good practice as an indicator of quality.

## Large-scale cascade models (including pilot and roll out)

There has been widespread recognition of the difficulties in ensuring a close match between the intentions of those who have designed an innovation and the messages received by those at its operational end. Cascade models of innovation were introduced to bring intended and received messages into closer alignment when attempts were being made to engage large numbers of teachers in a process of change. Often closely linked to resource-based models of dissemination, a cascade model generally involves a group of individuals being 'trained' in the subject to be disseminated. Having completed their own training programme, these trainees then become trainers responsible for training other groups of teachers. The training then cascades like a fountain or the pyramid model of sales in commerce. Major assessment developments throughout the UK in the 1980s and 1990s had aspects of the cascade model in-built. In such programmes development officers trained local authority personnel, who then trained teachers. In England, Stobart and Stoll (2005) identified the cascade model as central to ideas of dissemination for the national pilot of the Key Stage 3 Strategy.

Although 'training the trainers' cascade models have had some success, their inherent weakness lies in the layers of the cascade. Like the children's game, Chinese whispers, the more layers of people involved in telling and retelling the story, the more distorted the central messages are likely to become.

Another means of promoting larger-scale uptake of ideas by teachers is often referred to as 'pilot and roll out'. The strategy involves ideas being developed and tried out (piloted) in a number of schools. The purposes of the process of piloting can be varied; for example, to explore the practicability of ideas and activities or their likely level of support among the teaching profession. Piloting ideas with schools can also be seen by curriculum developers as a strategy to build credibility for a particular initiative, perhaps among policy makers or among teachers and schools. Ultimately, the desired message is that 'these ideas have been tried out in schools and have been seen to work'. The subsequent 'roll out' phase involves the transmission of ideas from the pilot schools to others. The positive evidence from teachers involved in the initial pilot is often used in the subsequent introduction of ideas to other teachers. In Scotland, the Reporting 5–14 initiative (SOEID, 1992) was developed using this model. At the time of its publication, this was an innovative model for reporting on pupils' progress to parents/carers. The model invited teachers to report levels of attainment and to write extended comments on children's strengths, areas for development and next steps. It was intended that this report would not only be used with parents but would also be passed on to the pupils' next teachers or next school. The model also proposed the creation of an agenda for parents' meetings, jointly constructed by teachers and parents with the next steps identified by teachers and supplemented by items for discussion identified by parents. Before publication the ideas from the policy were piloted in a number of schools and the findings from the pilot were used to adapt the policy statement and to build policy-related staff development materials. The policy itself was then rolled out to all schools, supported by evidence from the pilot phase.

## Unintentional dissemination

The models of dissemination described above all have a degree of intentionality in common; an intention to influence through the introduction of ideas to individuals and to groups. However, perhaps some of the most effective examples of dissemination arise not from strategic dissemination but from unintentional dissemination. For example, in Scotland national policy in assessment (SOED, 1991) was clear in its advice on how national tests (now known as national assessments) should be used in schools:

> Pupils should take a test at a given level of the 5–14 curriculum
> only when the teacher had already established with classroom

evidence, informal and formal, that she/he was able to demonstrate success across the defined strands of reading (or writing)
at that level. The function of the test should be simply to confirm the teacher's judgement on the basis of a much more limited
range of tasks than could be observed in class work.

(Hayward and Spencer, 2006: 226–7)

What actually happened was very different. National tests became high
stakes and in schools across the country teachers used tests not to confirm professional judgement but to substitute for it. There were countless
reports of schools rehearsing pupils for tests and stories of mass testing of
pupils at particular times of the year, commonly just before parents' meetings. There are interesting issues to be explored in examples like this. Why
did teachers appear to act against policy advice, particularly in a context
where it was argued that too often teachers merely conformed to policy?
And why act against a policy that recognized the importance of teachers'
professional judgement in ways that teachers wanted at the time?

Perhaps other things interfered. Perhaps the context for the assessment
policy appeared to be at odds with the policy itself and factors beyond
the planned process of dissemination created a received message that was
more powerful than the intended national policy message. Ozga and Jones
(2006) explore this issue using Jones and Alexiadou's (2001) distinction
between travelling and embedded policy. They argue that there is an increasingly global agenda, a 'travelling policy' (p. 2), among transnational
policy elites. They describe embedded policy as existing priorities and
practices. In this case it appears that the global context of performativ-
ity and the interpretation or misinterpretation of the actions of others;
for example, the collection by school inspectors during inspections of the
proportions of pupils achieving each level of attainment using test results,
may have led to teachers responding to what they perceived to be the
dominant rather than the local policy drivers.

Dissemination as transmission has had limited success but what, if any,
alternatives are there?

## Dissemination as transformation

In the late 1990s there was increasing unrest about the impact or lack
of impact of educational innovation on practice. For example, school inspectors in Scotland reported evidence that despite very positive reactions
to the ideas in the Assessment 5–14 policy, there had been little progress
in putting its ideas into practice. They recounted considerable variability

in the quality and consistency of the information teachers collected and reported to parents, pupils and other teachers (SOEID, 1991).

   In an attempt to bring into closer alignment ideas from research, policy and practice, alternative approaches to the dissemination of ideas have been explored. These ideas move beyond the concept of dissemination as transmission to explore how ideas might become embedded in ways that would transform practice, policy and research. Work in this area brought together research evidence from learning, teaching and assessment (e.g. Black and Wiliam, 1998a; Black, 2001; Harlen and Deakin Crick, 2002, 2003; Black et al., 2006b) with evidence from research on school improvement (e.g. Stoll and Fink, 1996), on school leadership (e.g. Swaffield and MacBeath, 2006) and on systems change (e.g. Fullan, 1993, 2003, 2004; Senge and Scharmer, 2001; Senge et al., 2005). This approach often described the process of change in exploratory terms such as 'travelling towards' and 'the journey', bringing together ideas of continuing professional learning, dissemination and sustainability into complex dynamic models. Models of dissemination designed to transform practice have begun to emerge across the UK, in small-scale projects such as the King's, Medway, Oxfordshire Formative Assessment, Project KMOFAP (Black et al., 2003) and in larger-scale projects such as Assessment is for Learning (AiFL) in Scotland; Assessment for Learning (AfL) in Wales and Northern Ireland and the Assessing Pupils' Progress (APP) in England (see Chapter 6). Although they were developed differently in different contexts, when thinking about how to extend ideas across schools, local authorities and countries, these projects had a number of features in common. First, they were concerned to identify crucial issues in learning. They recognized the need for impact in areas across the education system, research, policy and practice. They were concerned with a collaborative process of change. For example, Black et al. suggest that:

> The assumption made about LHTL [Learning How to Learn] in this project is that it is best seen in terms of a collection of good learning practices. In selecting these practices, we have judged that the evidence from a variety of empirical and theoretical studies supports the view that emphasis should be placed on practices, in both individual and collaborative contexts, that seem to have potential to promote pupils' autonomy in learning. This would seem to be the most secure foundation for lifelong learning. We believe that further understanding and insight in L2L [Learning to Learn] and LHTL is to be attained by engaging in development and research into a variety of such learning practices and into teachers' capacity to implement and support them. Insofar as teachers are also learners, and their schools can be described

as learning organizations, we believe that these insights may be equally applicable to learning at these levels also.

(Black et al., 2006b: 131)

Each project made explicit the assumptions underlying their approach to the process, offering examples of practice in what matters in learning supported by research evidence. Each acknowledged the need for collaborative engagement among teachers, policy makers and researchers to extend existing understanding, and recognized the importance of similar principles informing the development of the projects themselves.

For example, the AifL initiative attempted to bring research, policy and practice into closer alignment. This programme that began in 2001 was designed to build on research on learning, teaching and assessment and on the process of change carried out, for example, by Hutchinson and Hayward (2005), Fullan, (1993), and Senge and Scharmer (2001).

Emerging from a review of organizations, public and private, where transformational change was perceived to have taken place, Senge and Scharmer (2001) suggest that the process of transformational change involves:

- engaging people in the process of change to develop practical knowledge that is useful in their everyday lives;
- fostering relationships and collaboration across organizations and researchers;
- creating opportunities for collective reflection;
- leveraging progress in individual organizations through cross-institutional links to sustain transformative change.

Improved practices in learning were not, therefore, disseminated in any traditional sense of transmission. Transformation was perceived to be most likely to emerge through communities working together to create new knowledge, recognizing the complexity of that process as described by Senge and Scharmer (2001): 'knowledge creation is an intensely human, messy process of imagination, invention and learning from mistakes embedded in a web of human relationships' (p. 247).

In Scotland, the intended AifL model (Hayward et al., 2004) had three key features:

1. The initiative should focus on real issues important for the communities that would participate in it.
2. The programme should be inclusive, involving all relevant communities in its development and thus seeking to address issues that might inhibit valuable change, such as competing policy demands.

3.  AifL should recognize the complexity of the change process and should not seek simplistic models that would be unlikely to achieve meaningful change, such as informing teachers of research findings and expecting practice to change as a consequence of that act.

Evaluation evidence suggests that this transformative approach had widespread impact on practice, particularly in formative assessment. For example the evaluation reports from Kirton et al. (2007) and Condie et al. (2005) identified meaningful changes in teachers' classroom practices as a result of their involvement in AiFL. In a follow-up study with teachers and local policy makers, Hayward et al. (2005) sought to understand what had led to changed practices in formative assessment, ultimately suggesting a complex of factors, interpreted differently in individual contexts. They describe as 'salutary' the list of some of the key factors in the complexity of successful change in pedagogy that emerged from their study:

- educational integrity, what matters for learning, which is itself a complex idea;
- recognition by all the relevant communities of what this means;
- actual improvement of learning occurring;
- ensuring depth and breadth of understanding about what really matters and its implications for the roles of all the teaching, research and policy communities;
- the significance of personal conviction on the part of teachers, and their full professional participation in deciding action to take the development forward;
- openness, equality, sharing of issues, problems, solutions and professional expertise across all the communities involved, including teachers, school managers, local authority staff, development officers, national policy makers and policy promoters, and researchers and advisory staff;
- effective interaction and sharing among the communities, leading to real change in the classroom learning community, networking in teacher groups in school and the wider peer group, and consistent policy and advice from the policy and research representatives;
- ensuring that all the communities are fully informed in respect of in-depth understanding of learning and teaching principles, the nature of participative learning as a strategy for teachers' continuing professional development, and the need to be aware of one's own community's standpoints and priorities and those of the other communities involved;

- recognition that the change process is personal and different for different individuals and groups;
- avoidance of omission of any of these important interacting factors and oversimplified strategies, such as formulaic school development or improvement planning.

Hayward and Spencer argue that ideas of dissemination are misleading if they imply a process of engaging others in formative assessment that is different from the complex of factors described above. Rather than look for superficially simplified versions of complex systems, the research, policy and practice communities may have to learn to live with complexity and to attempt to develop deeper insights into the nature of the complexities.

> Our study suggests there are things that matter in the process of real change, things that matter whether an individual or a school is in the first phase of a development or the last and without which we will be forever condemned to push the boulder of innovation uphill only to have it roll back down.
>
> (Hayward and Spencer, 2006: 19)

## What matters in the growth of ideas beyond the classroom?

Traditional models of change have separated ideas of continuing professional development, pilot and roll out, dissemination and sustainability, and the result has been an alarming lack of impact. The language we use to describe the processes of educational change does not appear to have served us well. Terms such as development, roll out and dissemination suggest a process different from that of learning. They suggest a view that learning is what happens with those involved in the initial pilot study, those who are developing the case study or those who are developing the policy. Once the resource exists or the programme has been developed the model changes. Those to whom the ideas are rolled out or disseminated are more or less told what to do. They might reflect on the practical implications for their practice but they are implementing the learning of others rather than creating new knowledge and learning for themselves.

Arguably, the assumptions at the base of this approach are that one school or one classroom is largely the same as another. This grossly oversimplifies the complexity of classrooms and schools where, for example, changing one pupil can change the nature of a class, or changing one teacher can change the dynamic of a school. Each situation is unique and dynamic and any attempt to simplify the essential complexity of these learning environments is almost certainly doomed to failure. James and Brown (2005) argue for the need for many descriptive studies of the nature of complex learning and change. The use of the term 'descriptive' is an interesting one. Bruner (1996) argues for four essential components of effective learning:

1. agency: individuals taking more control of their own learning activity.
2. reflection: making what is being learned make sense, understanding it, internalizing it.
3. collaboration: sharing the resources of the 'mix of human beings' involved in teaching and learning, pupils, teachers.
4. culture: the construction by individuals and groups of particular ways of life and thought that they call reality.

He argues for the importance of narrative in helping us to understand our world and our part in it. Much of the more recent literature on the process of change has used the metaphor of the journey, recognizing that as an educational community we are at a very early stage in our own journey towards understanding. As Fullan (2003) put it: 'It is not a case of going down a road travelled before for the road has not yet been made. Travel and make the road' (p. 106).

It may be that if we are to do as Fullan suggests, and learn much more about what matters in developing and sharing ideas, then we need new ways of engaging in, and a new language to describe, these processes. Perhaps we need to explore the ecology of the process and to learn through the narratives and critical analyses of individuals and groups involved in learning to change. We may also need to recognize that we never move beyond individual or small group learning; we simply increase the numbers of people learning.

However, analysing the problems will only take us so far. The challenge remains how to bring together ideas from research, policy and practice in assessment on a large scale. If we think of dissemination as the purposeful growth of ideas within and across communities, it may be useful to reflect on the metaphor of a pool of water into which a stone of innovation is thrown. Black (2008) suggests that there are three questions that arise if we begin to think of the growth rather than the dissemination of ideas. What is the pool like? What is the stone like? What are the ripples that flow from the stone's initiation?

What then might the pool be like? The context, within which the innovation is to be situated, is likely to have a number of dimensions, personal, social and political. For example, a situation in which teachers perceive themselves to have been subjected to multiple innovations over time and who feel personally and professionally deskilled by the process is very different from one where teachers have been involved in the identification of an innovation as key to their own view of what matters in the enhancement of learning and teaching. A school where there has been a consistent history of commitment to supporting teachers in the exploration and development of ideas in their own contexts, which also includes having opportunities to work with others to develop their thinking, is different to one where teachers have been told their developmental priorities and judged on their ability to conform. A policy context that establishes educational priorities in partnership with other stakeholders and then seeks to promote policy coherence across different communities, curriculum, professional development and quality enhancement is different from one where policy is established centrally, disseminated nationally and assessed judgementally. It is unlikely that any context matches exactly any of these caricatures but any innovation seeking to have broad impact has to reflect honestly on the context within which the innovation will be situated and plan how to address the issues that the context may raise.

What might that mean in practice? The design of a dissemination strategy would have to include consideration of a wide range of issues; for example:

- the value positions of the participants;
- how different communities might be involved to promote coherence across research, policy and practice;
- the nature of what is being asked of people and their capacity to engage;
- the differing contexts within which innovations in assessment are likely to emerge.

The contexts of primary and secondary schooling may be very different, as may the national policy contexts in different parts of the UK.

What is the stone like? In this context the stone might simply be an analogy for the innovation in assessment. The reality, however, is more complicated. Any development in assessment is inexorably linked to curriculum and to pedagogy. In schools and classrooms, if the curriculum provides the broad boundaries through which progress in learning might be determined, then formative assessment is strongly associated with pedagogy, with approaches to learning and teaching designed to promote the greatest likelihood of success in learning. If the stone is innovation in assessment in schools, then pedagogy is equally important. In this case it would imply that the model of professional learning would be based on ideas of transformation, of participation and collaboration; and the design of the innovation would have to consider the nature of the pool into which the stone is to be thrown. The projects cited earlier offer some insights into models of professional learning that appear to offer the potential for greater impact. Ideas of participant engagement, shared purpose, collaboration, manageability and contextualization appear central.

The nature of the stone is also an issue. The debate in formative assessment about fidelity to the original ideas of what matters in formative assessment often emerges in debates about the relationship between the ideas and strategies used in schools. There is an argument that strategies are all too easily separated from ideas with formative assessment; for example, all too quickly becoming decontextualized strategies such as traffic lights, sharing (telling) criteria and wait time. Certainly, strategies used in classrooms without purpose have little to commend them. Brown and Campione (1996) argue that there is a point of lethal mutation at which the relationship between intention and practice is so tenuous that it becomes meaningless. Reeves (2007), on the other hand, argues that teachers' use of the language of strategies is complicated, reflecting the practical worlds they inhabit and acting as a shared code to explain ideas in context. There is more work to be done here, to develop deeper understanding of how the different languages of different communities may influence our understanding of one another's context.

Finally, there are the ripples. The impact of the innovation on the context might be seen to represent the growth of ideas more broadly throughout the system. One stone thrown into a pool creates a gentle pattern of ever-increasing circles influencing ever greater areas of the pool. The circles are similar but their numbers grow. In this context, dissemination would seek to increase continuously the numbers of people changing their practices until there comes a point at which new practices are regarded as the norm by most people, until the circles once again blend into the pool.

However, the idea of a gentle pool disturbed by a single stone from which circles radiate is not an image entirely consistent with recent national or international policy and practice. All four countries within the UK have experienced periods during which schools have been subjected to a barrage of initiatives. Throwing many stones into the pool has led to significant disruption with overlapping patterns becoming confused and difficult to discern. Many schools report such confusion. They perceive themselves to have been subjected to multiple initiatives with little coherence leading to feelings of overload and disempowerment among staff.

All educational communities, researchers, policy makers and practitioners have crucial roles to play in building assessment systems that will improve the life chances of young people. To do that we may have to ask hard questions of the reductionist systems of change that have recently dominated thinking and practice. The process of the growth of ideas across communities in ways that are likely to be sustainable still feels a little too much like the myth of Sisyphus in Ancient Greece.[1]

## Questions for reflection

1. Reflecting on a recent assessment innovation, to what extent was it well informed by research?

2. How did the plans for innovation in assessment link to curriculum and approaches to learning and teaching?

3. What roles did teachers, pupils, staff and parents play in the planning and development process?

4. What support did people need and how were such needs identified?

5. How did different communities support one another as the innovation developed?

6. To what extent did practice influence policy or policy influence practice?

7. What evidence was there that the innovation was making a positive difference?

8. To what extent were the strategies for evaluation consistent with the collaborative values of the process?

## Note

1. Sisyphus was condemned for eternity by Zeus to roll a large stone up a hill and to repeat the task as it rolled back down again on each occasion.

# 6 Professional learning to support teacher assessment

*Wynne Harlen*

Change in the assessment practice of teachers requires at the very least familiarity with new practices but hopefully leads to understanding their rationale and commitment to using them. This chapter looks at how teachers are introduced to new assessment approaches and procedures in a range of assessment reform projects, discussed in terms of a series of models of professional learning. From the examples, key aspects of the content and structure, which have to be considered in designing programmes for introducing new practices, are identified. These include differences according to the formative or summative purpose of the assessment, the balance of emphasis between principles and practice and between developing ownership through a 'bottom-up' approach and the uniformity of a 'top-down' approach. There is also a need to provide teachers with time for reflection and discussion among peers with feedback on their progress, and to make provision for different starting points and working environments. It must always be acknowledged, however, that teachers often work under constraints that prevent full implementation of changes they would like to make. In the short term the professional learning programme may therefore not lead to change in students' learning.

## Introduction

Using the term 'professional learning' instead of the more common one of professional development recognizes that an attempt to change practice in education must aim for a change in understanding rather than a superficial change in teaching techniques. This applies to assessment reform as much as to other changes in education. The content of the professional learning activities will differ according to the particular purpose of the intended change in assessment, but a common feature, whatever the focus, is the exchange of roles. Teachers become learners and assessors become the assessed. This does not necessarily mean that the approach is 'top-down' or that there is a simple recipe that teachers are trained to follow. What it does mean is that teachers understand the reasons for changes and are active in seeing how to implement them in their own particular working environment. This parallels the active role that students have in learning with understanding.

Practising teachers continue to learn in a variety of ways – from informal contact with other teachers to formal courses that lead to enhanced qualifications. Some learn from studying their own practice through action research or individually through mentoring, while most formal professional learning takes place in groups. Teachers also learn from both giving and receiving information about their practice to their peers at conferences and in-service meetings, and they learn from researchers and teacher educators in courses focused on particular issues or changes.

The practices of formative assessment and summative assessment using teachers' judgements demand skills that differ considerably from those of traditional teaching and testing. When first introduced they are unlikely to be developed through informal teachers' learning routes and will require some structured opportunities to consider evidence and approaches to change. Here we look at different models of professional learning and then consider the procedures used in various assessment reform projects, to find out what has been done in particular circumstances, what seemed to work well, what was less successful, and why, and what conclusions can be drawn.

## Degrees of implementation of change

Change in teachers' understanding and practice can take place to varying degrees. In the case of curriculum change, implementation has been described as taking place at a number of levels. Rudduck and Kelly (1976), studying the implementation of new curriculum materials in the early 1970s, identified a dimension ranging from 'awareness' to 'commitment'. At the 'awareness' end are teachers who know about the new materials but have yet to adopt their use. At the 'commitment' end are those who have become convinced of the value of the new materials and fully understand their rationale. In between these are teachers who use the new materials, at first somewhat mechanically and then with growing understanding of their purpose.

A similar range of degrees of change no doubt exists in relation to new assessment practices, which is our focus here. Here, too, effective implementation may involve giving up existing practices and a change in the role of the teacher. Unless there is commitment supported by thorough understanding, it is all too easy for new practices to fade away when there are competing demands for attention. So, in considering the effectiveness of different approaches to professional learning, we take evidence of the degree to which there is informed commitment to change as an indication of the extent of 'success'.

## Models of professional learning

Experience in many areas of change in education, be it in the curriculum, pedagogy, assessment or school organization and management, is that participation in developing new procedures or materials is a most effective way of encouraging commitment to change. When groups of teachers work together with researchers or developers, they can be creative and experimental in a safe environment, learn from each other, combine ideas and achieve ownership of the emerging practices in what is described as a 'bottom-up' approach. Add opportunities to reflect and develop understanding of principles underlying the change and this experience can be a most effective form of professional learning. But it is also very demanding of resources, particularly time, and clearly cannot easily be extended to large numbers of teachers. It does, however, indicate the kinds of experience that are likely to be effective in cases where change requires more than adopting new techniques.

Beyond the development phase, when the aim is to reach large numbers of teachers, the approaches to professional learning must be capable of being scaled up. The opportunities to involve teachers in genuine development are clearly limited. In large-scale dissemination programmes, there is less opportunity to tailor experiences to individual needs. However, the content and structure can still support collaborative learning that enables teachers to put new ideas into practice in the context of their own school and classroom. For example, the opportunity for teachers to visit each other's classrooms or to show videos of their teaching (Frederiksen and White, 1994) has been found effective in enhancing teachers' learning, and with appropriate funding can be built into professional learning programmes.

The role of the professional learning provider is central and itself may have to be the subject of development and change. Materials for professional learning providers, which spell out the procedures and provide materials for discussion and trial, can enable teachers to develop some ownership of the classroom actions that emerge, but replication of the experience of development is limited because the course of the professional learning activities has to be predetermined. The nearest approach is through experiences that start from the need for change, provide some strategies and examples, and encourage teachers to adapt them to their own work. Alternatives are to present teachers with more closely defined classroom techniques to be tried, adapted or to be followed according to their particular starting points, a 'top-down' approach.

These variations can be expressed as a series of models, differing in the extent to which teachers can have genuine participation in the development of new materials or practices. Here they are arranged roughly in order of 'bottom-up' to 'top-down'.

A. *Full participation:* Involving teachers genuinely in the development of ways of implementing change. In this case the starting points are evidence of the need for change and the aims that guide how this need is addressed. As noted above, this is known to be highly motivating and encourages development of understanding of the principles in order to create solutions to problems.

B. *Simulated participation:* Providing teachers with experiences that replicate the involvement in development, in order to provide motivation and understanding, even though strategies for the kinds of change in classroom practice that are required have already been identified. Teachers' professional learning experiences retain some of the openness of genuine development, as in model A, full participation, but are designed to avoid blind alleys. Examples are workshop activities where teachers study scenarios of classroom practice and work out where changes may be needed to achieve certain aims, such as helping students to implement self- and peer-assessment.

C. *Trial and adjustment:* Providing classroom materials or activities, designed by others, for teachers to try out in their classrooms and evaluate in relation to the aims. This gives opportunity for development of the activities and their evaluation encourages the teachers' exploration of the underlying principles.

D. *Practice of techniques:* Providing opportunities to learn about and practise techniques, involving precise instructions on the nature of changes that they are intended to implement. Training in the use of new teaching aids, such as using an interactive white board, or software for student records, often takes this form, but it has been used to introduce procedures, such as those for the 'numeracy' and 'literacy' hours in England, when large numbers of teachers have to be trained in a short time.

How far each of these approaches leads to understanding the principles behind the new practices may depend on several cross-cutting variables. One of these is the kind of rationale that is given for making the change. This can be highly pragmatic: 'because it works and leads to better learning'; or alternatively 'because this is how it works and leads to better learning'. For instance, in the case of formative assessment, the starting rationale for most recent projects has been the research evidence from Black and Wiliam's (1998a) review of classroom assessment. This 'because it works' reason is good enough in many cases, although it does not lead to the understanding of principles behind the advocated practices. Moving on to the question 'why does it work?' is more likely to lead to the understanding needed for a commitment to change, which in turn is likely to be more robust in the face of competing demands.

Other variables can affect the choice of approach that is most appropriate and feasible in a certain context and these include the:

- extent of the implementation (a few schools, a local authority or nation-wide);
- content focus (how novel is the intended change);
- target (individual teachers, groups or whole schools);
- timescale and time available for teachers to reflect and share;
- funds available.

Combining the various approaches to changing classroom practice with varying grasps of the underlying principles leads to Sarason's (1971) 'universe of alternatives' of the ways of enabling teachers to change. More than one approach may be used in a particular professional learning programme. For example, model D, practice of techniques, may be best for giving information about new practices, but for teachers to try out and reflect on how they can change their own practice requires the opportunities provided in model B, simulated participation. This can become model A, full participation, if teachers are encouraged to work out their own solutions on how to make changes.

Each of the many approaches rests either explicitly or implicitly on a view of teacher learning. To oversimplify for the sake of illustration, models A and B appear to place emphasis on social interaction and teachers learning from each other. They enable teachers to find the best way of achieving the aims in their own classrooms through peer evaluation and sharing experiences. They are based essentially on a social constructivist view of learning, where change is seen as something that is brought about through teachers' own collaborative thinking (see Lave and Wenger, 1991). Model C, trial and adjustment, is also based on a constructivist view but depends more on individual experience and reflection. There is an assumption that adult learning is similar to students' learning and that reflection on how they have developed understanding will enable them to understand how their students learn.

The fourth approach, model D, practice of techniques, is driven by a behaviourist view of learning, in which Bransford et al. (1999) argue learning is conceptualized 'as a process of forming connections between stimuli and responses' (p. 6). It is still widely used, for example, in the USA, where some teaching and professional learning materials are closely prescribed and may even dictate what the professional learning facilitators are to say. Teachers attending workshops primarily learn how to use new materials or procedures, leaving the building of their understanding of the change until later, or not at all.

## The assessment context

The points above draw on experience in curriculum change, which has a greater corpus of better documentation to date than change in assessment. The focus on change in assessment practice raises some fresh questions. For example:

- Does the implementation of assessment for formative purposes require greater change in pedagogy than implementation of change in assessment by teachers for summative purposes?
- How does change in assessment for either formative or summative purposes affect change in the other?
- How do the various summative purposes of assessment affect what can be done?
- To what extent do the demands of parents, students, employers and others for qualifications, and society for information about effectiveness of schools, affect the autonomy of teachers in relation to what and how assessment is carried out?

These questions relate to issues beyond professional learning by encompassing other aspects of bringing about change, such as how impact is evaluated and sustained, which are considered in other chapters of this book. We return to them in relation to professional learning after looking at examples of the form that professional learning has taken in a selection of the assessment reform projects examined under auspices of the ARIA study.

## Examples of professional learning in a selection of assessment reform projects

### The King's Medway Oxfordshire Formative Assessment Project (KMOFAP)

The KMOFAP was the forerunner of several recent projects developing the formative use of assessment or assessment for learning (AfL) and is therefore worthy of discussing first. KMOFAP started soon after Black and

Wiliam (1998a) completed their review of classroom research and recognized the importance of finding ways in which teachers could incorporate formative assessment into their work. Advisory staff from the Oxfordshire and Medway local authorities became partners with King's College staff in planning work with two mathematics and two science teachers from each of six secondary schools. The funding enabled teachers to be released for in-service sessions comprising seven whole-day and one half-day sessions spread over 18 months. The aim of the earlier sessions was for teachers to draw up action plans for implementation in the subsequent school year. According to Wiliam et al. (2004), the first six months was a time for the teachers to: 'experiment with some of the strategies and techniques suggested by the research, such as rich questioning, comment-only marking, sharing criteria with learners, and student peer-assessment and self-assessment' (p. 54).

During the project, team members visited teachers' classrooms to observe and discuss what was happening and how it related to the action plans. These visits were described by Wiliam et al. as 'not directive, but more like holding up a mirror to the teachers' (p. 54). The input to the teachers was thus designed to engage them in identifying how to put various features of formative assessment into practice. The teachers were introduced to general strategies and some idea of what to aim for, but not given models of what to do. This was an unusual and perhaps uncomfortable role for the teachers to be given by researchers and advisers who they regarded as experts. Wiliam recorded it in the following manner:

> At first, it seems likely that the teachers did not believe this. They seemed to believe that the researchers were operating with a perverted model of discovery learning in which the researchers knew full well what they wanted the teachers to do, but didn't tell them, because they wanted the teachers 'to discover it for themselves'. However, after a while, it became clear that there was no prescribed model of effective classroom actions, and each teacher would need to find their own way of implementing these general principles in their own classrooms.
>
> (Wiliam et al., 2004: 51)

The approach thus most closely resembles model A, full participation, in relation to change in classroom practice. In relation to the understanding of underlying principles and how the different practice was expected to impact on learning, there was a change during the series of in-service sessions.

In trying out the activities in practice, the teachers became aware of the need to understand why these particular activities are important and why they 'work', thus leading them to the underlying theoretical ideas. The theory that brings these together and provides a rationale for their adoption refers to a particular view of learning, one in which learners take an active part. Thus the researchers found that as teachers used the activities and saw the reaction of their students to them, they wanted to know more about the way students learn. So, approximately a year after starting the work focusing on classroom actions, one of the in-service sessions was designed to introduce teachers to theories of learning. Black et al. (2003) recognized that they could have worked in a reverse direction, by starting from the theory, explaining the kind of learning that the activities were designed to promote and then setting about developing the activities that would fit the requirements of this kind of learning. Thus, the same model could be applied with different types of rationale. In this case it moved from the pragmatic to the principled at the request of the teachers.

## How effective was the intervention?

In terms of a strategy for transforming research findings into classroom practices, Black et al. (2003) reported that the new practices developed by teachers were 'far more rich and more extensive than those we were able to suggest at the outset of the project on the basis of the research literature. All of them involve(d) change in the way that they work with their students and with the curriculum' (p. 57).

In terms of change in teachers, there were the expected differences in response among the 24 teachers. There was a variation in the number of ideas relating to formative assessment (e.g. questioning, feedback, sharing goals and criteria with students, student self-assessment) that the teachers undertook to develop in their classrooms. However, the researchers reported changes in several respects in all of the teachers involved in the project. In particular they noted change in:

- the way teachers thought of their goal as being to help students learn, in contrast to 'getting through the curriculum';
- the teachers' expectations of their students, in that all were able to learn given time and the right approach;
- teachers giving students more control and sharing with them the responsibility for learning.

Black et al. (2003) claimed that the changes in practice were slow to appear but were lasting, and that they were unlikely to have occurred had the researchers provided recipes for successful lessons. They considered that 'the change in beliefs and values are the result of the teachers casting themselves as learners and working with us to learn more' (p. 98).

In terms of change in students' learning, Black et al. (2003) reported that 'even when teachers used only one or two of the ideas of formative assessment, this did have an impact on their students' achievement' (p. 81). Evidence to support improved learning was detailed by Wiliam et al. (2004). Using a variety of comparison classes and internal school examinations, Key Stage 3 national curriculum assessments or GCSE results as outcome measures, they reported after only one year of the intervention:

> We believe the results . . . provide firm evidence that improving formative assessment does produce tangible benefits in terms of externally mandated tests (such as Key Stage 3 tests and GCSE examinations in England). Placing a quantitative estimate on the size of the effect is difficult but it seems likely that improvements equivalent to approximately one-half of a GCSE grade per subject are achievable.
>
> (Wiliam et al., 2004: 63)

In relation to the range of evidence used for formative assessment, one of the notable findings was that the secondary teachers could not ignore tests in developing their practice. Black et al. (2003) had initially tried to keep formative assessment separate from summative, but eventually concluded that 'it is unrealistic to expect teachers and students to practise such separation, so the challenge is to achieve a more positive relationship between the two' (p. 55). The main ways in which teachers used summative tests formatively were in helping students to prepare for tests, through revision, preparing their own tests and using the results of tests to feed back into teaching.

## Portsmouth Learning Community: Assessment for Learning Strand

Information about this project is mainly taken from the evaluation report by Blanchard et al. (2004). The formal professional development took the form of two teachers from each school attending three training days with Shirley Clarke, an educational consultant,[1] over the period of a year. The report was based on interviews with teachers and pupils in spring 2004 and observations during the in-service days.

The in-service days provided teachers with classroom techniques such as sharing learning intentions, identifying success criteria, no-hands-up questioning, comments-only marking and discussion with a partner. As a result Blanchard et al. reported that all the teachers made positive use of the ideas for AfL and that:

> . . . many changes to classroom practice have been made in what has been a dynamic and evolving process. There were significant

indications that the teachers grew in confidence and authority through their process of experimentation and reflection.

(Blanchard et al., 2004: 2)

The report describes in considerable detail the changes reported by the teachers and helpfully combines some of these changes into two forms of AfL implementation, which they describe as 'transparent' and 'interactive' learning environments.

'Transparent' describes a classroom where goals are made explicit and teachers find out and try to promote pupils' ideas through their questioning. The emphasis moves from being focused on activities to being focused on what teachers want pupils to learn. However, the process is essentially teacher-controlled; the pupils: '... cannot be said to 'own' the learning, and they tend not to engage actively with the learning intentions other than to accept them implicitly and act on them'. (Blanchard et al., 2004: 4)

'Interactive' is used to describe a classroom in which pupils play a far greater part in decisions than in a 'transparent' classroom. Pupils actively discuss the purposes of what they do and their progress; there is much more emphasis on self-evaluation than in the 'transparent' classroom. Learning is more pupil-driven than teacher-driven. While transparency 'aims to improve learning by using assessment to enable all pupils to perform better', in interactivity there is an aim for 'assessment to support all pupils' learning how to learn'.

Blanchard et al. (2004) use the extent of interactivity as a measure of success in teaching: 'The more pupils play an active part in decision-making about processes, the more interactive we would say their learning is, and the more successful the teaching' (p. 12).

This implies a development from 'prescription', a learning environment in which teachers do not share goals and success criteria with pupils, to transparency and then to interactivity. Presumably, the further along this development the more successful is the professional learning in promoting formative assessment. The researchers do not attempt to quantify the change that may have taken place towards these types of classroom environments, but they do claim that all teachers involved avoided prescription. They also suggest, however, that a minority of teachers were involving pupils in defining the focus of their activities.

The researchers identified another dimension of change, relating to how far teachers integrated assessment into teaching. There were teachers who saw formative assessment as 'reinforcing the guiding principles the school had articulated' and others who saw the 'challenge as one of incorporating into their existing repertoire of teaching methods what AfL's supporters recommend' (p. 3). They recorded a variety of evidence as indicating implementation of AfL including:

- change in teachers' planning;
- sharing with pupils an overview of a term's work as well as lesson intentions;
- the use of 'traffic lights';
- teachers' greater clarity about what to teach and freedom to decide how to teach it;
- recognizing the importance of pupils talking about their work;
- awareness of the need to provide pupils with ways of finding help when they were stuck.

These suggest that the teachers understood that pupils should be in charge of their learning. In terms of the models of professional learning, Blanchard et al. (2004) suggested that '. . . the spirit of the project was to consider the value of recommended AfL strategies, to trial their use in the classroom, to reflect on the effects and to discuss developments with other colleagues (p. 7).

In some schools whole-school training days were devoted to AfL and support from the school management was one of the factors mentioned as supporting the implementation of AfL. However, the aim of the project was for the strategies to be trialled in the classrooms of the two teachers involved, who usually worked together, rather than the whole school. The professional learning experience was closest to model C, trial and adjustment, but as the following excerpts imply, the style of the three input days may have been prescriptive, bordering on model D, practice of techniques:

> It is possible that the style used to deliver training gave the impression that there were classroom procedures that had been found to be successful and that ought to be followed (p. 17).

> Sometimes well-meaning authoritative outsiders to the classroom, in their desire to pass on to teachers what research has found, can strain too hard and turn complex, contexted, dynamic issues into urgent prescription and imperative (p. 20).

> A small number of teachers expressed concern about possible dangers in creating too strict an orthodoxy in the use of AfL. Some commented on the discomfort they felt that adhering to strict formulae for learning intentions and success criteria ran the risk of inhibiting vital flexibility in the teachers' response to individual pupils' needs and events as they occurred (p. 17).

It can also be inferred that the formal in-service days provided techniques but did not communicate the underlying principles. For example, there was some reported confusion about the purpose of techniques such as 'no hands up' and difficulty in developing success criteria with the pupils. Unless techniques are very tightly specified – more than is really possible in general strategies for use in formative assessment – teachers have to make decisions and are left uncertain as to how to do this unless they have an understanding of the rationale.

The changes that were reported raise the issue of where professional learning experience begins and ends. In this case it certainly did not end with the three in-service days, for clearly the pairs of teachers continued to explore classroom activities for AfL from other publications, those of the Assessment Reform Group being mentioned. It was also evident that they found the researchers' interviews helpful: 'Many reported that the opportunity to talk to others had helped them to clarify issues and successes, and particularly appreciated the researchers' visits' (p. 16).

The Blanchard et al. (2004) report noted that teachers found it particularly helpful 'to talk without feeling that there is a right or wrong answer'. This echoes the value that pupils found in being able to talk with peers.

It appears that the possible prescriptive nature of the professional learning was offset by opportunities for working with other teachers who were also trying to implement change and for discussion with outsiders. It is certainly clear that professional learning does not end with the formal in-service sessions. Opportunities for teachers to meet and talk about their experiences and to develop a shared understanding of what they have tried and found in their classrooms is itself a professional learning experience nearer to model B, simulated participation.

## Kings Oxfordshire Summative Use of Assessment Project (KOSAP)

This project was designed to find an approach to summative assessment that would have fewer negative effects on teachers and pupils than the tests currently in operation in England. The aim was 'to develop methods and processes for ensuring the comparability of judgements between teachers and schools, to investigate the reliability and validity of these judgements, and to disseminate the findings to a variety of audiences' (see website: King's College, 2009). In its pilot phase, the project worked with a small group of Year 8 English and mathematics teachers, all well-versed in formative assessment practices. It focused on the process of making summative judgements and how evidence is turned into judgements. The development was initiated by teachers identifying 'what does it mean to be good at this subject for Year 8?', clearly a bottom-up approach involving teachers in developing new ideas (model A, full participation). In the second phase during the school year 2005/6 new practices were tried out and adapted (model B, simulated participation). The third phase involved the teachers spreading the ideas and practices across their departments.

The findings of the pilot project, derived from field notes, class observations, interviews and records of meetings, indicated some misunderstandings about summative assessment. These included confusion between formative and summative assessment and acceptance rather than challenge of the quality of current tests. If these are widespread issues, it is clearly important to address such matters in professional learning when extending new summative assessment practice to schools. Other findings, echoing similar ones in relation to formative assessment, were differences between the reactions of teachers of mathematics and English.

Teachers of English were reported to be comfortable with a portfolio system similar to current practice, placing greater emphasis on speaking and listening and also preferring to introduce a 'controlled' piece of work, on which students worked alone. Mathematics teachers preferred to keep to the use of tests but to improve them, or to introduce 'alternative assessment tasks' rather than a more holistic approach that was favoured by the English teachers. However, the mathematics approach was found not to provide pupils with opportunities to show a range of achievement, which came as a surprise to the teachers when they became aware of it. This highlights another aspect to be addressed in professional learning, to counteract the finding that some mathematics teachers queried the need for change.

## Summative teacher assessments at the end of Key Stage 2

This project, which began in 2006, was prompted by the Assessment Reform Group's Assessment Systems for the Future Project (ARG, 2006) and aimed to provide an alternative model for statutory end-of-key-stage teachers' assessment and moderation. Over a six-month period, meetings were held with a small group of Year 6 teachers from the City of Birmingham and Oxfordshire local authorities. These teachers were in the process of conducting their end of Key Stage 2 judgements and meetings of the group were used to moderate these processes and reflect on their experience of different ways of doing this. Prior to the project many teachers were basing their assessment on giving their pupils past national tests. Teachers, in collaboration with local authority advisers, developed materials to help the process of basing judgements on a broad range of relevant evidence drawn from pupils' regular work. These materials included:

- guidance for the summative use of assessment of reading, writing and mathematics, including 'assessment focuses' linked to national curriculum level descriptions;

- suggestions for sources of evidence in the form of 'jigsaws' indicating the most important and readily available;
- principles underpinning an alternative model of teachers' assessment and moderation processes (similar in some respects to the principles in Chapter 2 although developed quite independently);
- prompts for evaluating and reviewing the school's processes for end-of-key stage teachers' assessment.

The materials were made available to a larger group of Year 6 teachers from 24 schools who took part in the project in 2007. The teachers collected evidence over a period of two terms and brought examples to two meetings where their judgements were moderated in discussion with other teachers. The meetings not only gave them direct experience of moderation but also gave them an opportunity to share their experiences, and then discuss their selections of evidence. In the first meeting, it was clear that most but not all of the 'principles' were being applied but less use was made of the 'jigsaws' in the selection of evidence. Perhaps surprisingly, they were more aware of using summative judgements to help further learning than they were of using the formative evidence to make summative judgements. They saw little role for pupils in the summative use of assessment. By the time of the second meeting, however, there were indications that the teachers were beginning to widen their evidence base, suggesting some professional learning through involvement in moderation. There was also some appreciation of the case for involving pupils.

The professional learning for these teachers might be categorized as model A, full participation, for the first phase (2006) and B, simulated participation, for the second (2007). The reaction of teachers to the experience of collaborative moderation was highly positive. They thought that all teachers should have such opportunities. While they valued the experience of full participation for themselves, they suggested that for wider dissemination the process would have to be 'formalized', which would inevitably move it towards the more top-down approaches of C or D.

## Formative assessment in the States of Jersey

Several developments were in progress in the early 2000s in the States of Jersey, stemming from a major conference in 2001 at which discussion with Paul Black and Dylan Wiliam led to a formal AfL initiative in collaboration with a team of researchers at King's College. At the same time as the formative assessment project (Jersey Actioning Formative Assessment (JAFA)), other initiatives were in progress, including an evaluation of a pilot study involving teacher assessment replacing Key Stage 1, 2 and 3 standard tests, and training for teachers in 'critical thinking skills'. The policy seemed to be to keep these various projects apart, using different classes and schools for trials. Inevitably, however, there was some mixing, especially as many schools were keen to participate in both the formative assessment and summative assessment projects. They used the King's College 'Black Box' publications (Black and Wiliam, 1998b; Black et al., 2002) for formative assessment and began exploring teachers' summative assessment ahead of formal involvement in the summative assessment project. Presumably, the intended separation was to prevent overload, but those teachers involved in more than one project saw how one supported another. In particular, Richardson's (2005) report on the summative teachers' assessment pilot showed that the most successful implementation was in schools also implementing formative assessment and critical skills.

Three different groups of schools took part in the formative assessment project, starting in three successive years from 2003. The evaluation by Crossouard and Sebba was published in 2006, so the third cohort was only part-way through when the evaluation data were collected. The evaluation selected six schools from across the three cohorts for one-day visits. During the visits the 'lead' teacher and senior management were interviewed, two classes were observed and discussions were held with the teachers and pupil focus groups. Documents relating to assessment policies were also analysed. Other schools were able to have their views represented by attending focus group meetings. No sessions given by visiting researchers were observed but information about them was obtained in the interviews.

As in the Portsmouth project, the professional learning provision was complex. At its core were in-service days for 'lead' teachers (one from each school), who were to bring the AfL work into the school and spread it within the school, a form of the cascade model discussed in Chapter 5. In addition, there were conferences for head teachers organized by the King's team; a conference for all teachers, two one-day in-service sessions given by the consultant Shirley Clarke and twilight sessions on various AfL topics during visits of the King's team.

Different models of professional learning were represented here. From Crossouard and Sebba's report, it seems that the King's team mostly adopted model B, simulated participation, in their sessions with the lead teachers.

> The input of the King's workshops was recognized as being different from other 'training courses', in the sense of not 'telling people what to do'. There was a mixed response to this. The advantages of letting schools work the ideas through their practice was recognized, but some felt it was not practical enough, or to lack direction [sic].
>
> (Crossouard and Sebba, 2006: 6)

The evaluation shows the difficulty of implementing model B, which can appear to leave teachers dissatisfied and having to fall back on their own ideas, even though this is exactly what was intended and likely to be of benefit in the longer term. Crossouard and Sebba (2006) commented that: 'Unless ownership of AfL initiatives is devolved to teachers, this may make it more likely that efforts to encourage AfL practices are experienced as 'top-down' rather than 'bottom up' initiatives' (p. 11).

The sessions offered by Shirley Clarke appeared to use model D, providing ideas and techniques that could be immediately used in the classroom. However, Crossouard and Sebba noted that: 'Some teachers dismissed the language used by Shirley Clarke as jargon that seemed "gimmicky"' (p. 6) and that inputs from teachers in England, who were part of the King's team, were not thought by the Jersey teachers to be helpful: 'Some schools felt that their own practice was already ahead of that described in presentations, particularly where they had begun to develop AfL drawing upon King's publications before the JAFA initiative' (p. 6).

These reactions may serve only to underline that it is difficult to please everyone. However, the teachers' reactions are a key source of evidence as to how successful the various professional learning inputs were. Other evidence from class observations and pupil reactions indicates that this cocktail of professional learning inputs had a positive effect on lesson management, the use of AfL strategies and on teachers' responses to pupils' needs. Pupils were articulate about learning and appeared to be engaged with it.

Evidence from focus groups and interviews showed the importance attached by the teachers to:

- local support from advisers for ongoing work: sustained support rather than occasional 'high level' inputs from 'experts';
- local 'vision': keeping the improvement of the whole of education in view;
- flexibility allowed in the use of funding for the initiative;
- the opportunity, provided by the cohort structure of the initiative, for professional dialogue among teachers;
- feedback on how they are doing (which some felt was lacking from the King's team);
- time, through provision of supply cover, for teachers to meet to review and audit their practice.

Overall, it was expenditure on human resources rather than written materials that provided best value.

Crossouard and Sebba reported the teachers' perceptions of the relationship between the requirements of AfL and developing critical skills as follows:

> Where AfL combined with critical skills, excitement and engagement were noted. In these situations, synergies between AfL and critical skills created a focus on social relations and learning processes . . .
>
> The emphasis on working in groups through critical skills facilitated peer assessment in AfL . . .
>
> Both initiatives encouraged dialogue about learning and contributed to pupils' ability to articulate their ideas about learning.
> (Crossouard and Sebba, 2006: 14)

The conclusion is not that the input from outsiders was not helpful but that a variety of inputs is needed and was in fact requested by schools. The importance of spreading the development within the school as a way of developing ownership was recognized. Moreover, the teachers in the first and second cohorts recognized the need to continue to develop practice, while the third cohort was concerned that they too should be allowed more time to develop their own practice rather than feeling that they were being 'done to'.

There was also some worry about the future and whether support for certain initiatives would be sustained, or decisions reversed. This suggests that openness in policy planning is important to sustaining change.

Crossouard and Sebba (2006) helpfully summarize the facilitating and inhibiting factors in relation to the development of AfL and make some recommendations. None of the identified factors directly related to the professional learning in the project, but there were several recommendations with implications for further activities that involve extending professional learning. The main factors are:

- Continued flexible funding to allow schools to develop the work through opportunities to share practice, observe other teachers, visit other schools etc;
- Allowing time for implementation of what are quite profound changes in policies and classroom culture using 'frequent drip-feed' and recognizing that schools are at different stages of change;
- Providing professional learning for teaching assistants including access to more formal training;
- Providing opportunities for lead teachers to undertake action research and further study (for masters or doctoral degrees).

# Implementing new assessment practice at national levels

Apart from the work in changing formative and summative assessment practice in Jersey, the projects so far discussed were restricted to a relatively small number of schools. However, projects intended to change practice across all schools in each of the four countries of the UK were also in progress. In Scotland, Wales and Northern Ireland, the changes in assessment were part of wider national programmes of educational change (see Chapter 3). For example, in Scotland, the formative assessment project was part of a bigger AifL programme that considered a whole assessment system – pupils' records, personal planning, system monitoring and school evaluation, as well as formative assessment and summative assessment at the classroom level. In Wales, following the decision to discontinue statutory national testing and replace it with teacher summative assessment alone, exploratory work aimed at strengthening teachers' assessment was undertaken in 13 local education authorities across Wales; the aim being to move away from unnecessary pupil 'levelling' or the levelling of individual pieces of work. At the same time, between 2005–2008, the Department for Children, Education, Lifelong Learning and Skills (DCELLS) set up and funded a programme focusing on developing thinking and assessment for learning in the classroom. In this section we use past and current reports on these national projects to pick out what is relevant to understanding the issues arising in providing professional learning on a large scale.

## Scotland

The professional learning provided in the AifL formative assessment project took a variety of forms, implied rather than made explicit in the report on the project by Hayward et al. (2005). Mention is made of national conferences, local workshops, presentations by Dylan Wiliam of King's College, presentations by teachers from the KMOFAP project in England and from Scottish teachers as the project progressed. There were also less formal, but nevertheless planned, discussions among local teachers and with education authority development officers. Some reference was also made to the King's College Black Box publications. Although visiting researchers were included in the professional learning programme, there is a clear impression that their participation was decided, designed and controlled in Scotland, rather than being a formal collaboration with those developing formative assessment in England or elsewhere.

Whether or not the range of professional learning activities that was provided was designed with the varying needs of different teachers in mind, it turned out to cater well for the several ways in which teachers came to implement formative assessment in their own practice. The Hayward et al. report describes three different routes to understanding how formative assessment can improve learning. The first suggests model C, trial and adjustment.

> Some teachers were enthused by the credibility of practitioners from the KMOFAP project, were encouraged to try out practical ideas in their own classrooms and became convinced of their efficacy by their impact on young people's learning and behaviour. Reflection on these experiences led these teachers to understand more deeply ideas from research on assessment and learning.
>
> (Hayward et al., 2005: 51)

Another group started from aims and ideas, suggesting model B, simulated participation: 'They talked through ideas with colleagues – teachers, head teachers, development officers or researchers – and then tried out strategies in practice' (p. 51).

A third group took the ideas and developed their own ways of incorporating them into their practice (model A, full participation) 'with renewed enthusiasm for their own professionalism' (p. 51).

Despite the different models used, the report identified some commonalities that appeared to motivate all teachers to take formative assessment seriously:

- a stimulus to engage, either through listening to practitioners or to researchers [with views] that connected with their own ideas about what matters in learning;
- practical suggestions about how to try out formative assessment, often allowing existing practice to be adapted;
- opportunities to talk through ideas with others;
- a sense of being listened to, of being important;
- early success in seeing a positive difference in children's learning;
- involvement in a practical, local development that gave a sense of contributing to a bigger endeavour;
- a perception of consistency of purpose across communities, e.g. individual, school, EA, HMIE, SEED.

(Hayward et al., 2005: 51–2)

Although there is a general impression of successful implementation by those in the project, the report comments on the apparent reluctance of some teachers to engage with theories of learning in order to understand why the strategies worked to enhance learning. It is possible, as Hayward et al. (2005) speculate, that rather than an explicit reference to theory, there was an 'in-depth practical understanding... amounting to an unarticulated theory of classroom practice based on one's own developing experience' (p. 57). This is may be what Cooper and McIntrye (1996) described as 'craft knowledge'. It could be expecting more than is reasonable for classroom teachers to engage with theory, but without it there is a risk that formative assessment remains a set of useful strategies rather than an indication of implementing a 'principled approach to all teaching'. Some teachers were reported as using just some of the strategies suggested, which may indicate a superficial grasp of what formative assessment is about. On the other hand, as those involved in providing professional learning pointed out, 'one has to begin somewhere'.

Hayward et al. (2005) also found that '... in all interviews it was clear that teachers did not engage the languages of or use higher order theories about learning' (p. 68). That is, there was no movement within a particular model from a pragmatic to a principled rationale. A teacher was quoted as generalizing that teachers do not want the theory, but rather the practical ideas to take away and try. It was certainly evident that the motivating factor most frequently mentioned by teachers was hearing at conferences the experiences of other teachers who reported that the ideas they had tried 'worked'. The meaning of 'worked' seemed to be that teachers were more aware of their pupils' thinking and understanding, and had a focus on learning rather than teaching. Thus, the teachers were aware of change in their teaching, and the researchers described the programme as encouraging them to 'grow professionally'.

However, in relation to the two forms of implementation offered by the evaluators of the Portsmouth project, the evidence presented suggests that in Scotland the learning environments were best described as 'transparent'. While pupils were taking more initiative in solving problems and were reported as doing more thinking and being clearer about what they should be learning, the teachers maintained a prescriptive grip on the lesson objectives. Teachers had ownership of the learning rather more than pupils, as would be found in a 'participative' environment. Of the hundreds of responses analysed by the researchers, only two explicitly described pupils taking part in deciding what their targets should be. Others were telling pupils about their goals rather than sharing the process of deciding goals.

This raises the question as to whether there was something missing in the professional learning that might account for the teachers going no further towards giving pupils more responsibility for their learning and being satisfied to do what 'works' without wanting to know why. However, the report revealed several features of the professional learning that were perceived as being effective.

Initial fears, identified in the earlier evaluation report by Kirton et al. (2007), that formative assessment practices would extend learning time and prevent teachers from covering the required curriculum content, were not realized as time went on. Small-scale workshops were found far more helpful than large ones. Teachers also made the point that it was most helpful to talk with other teachers from the same phase and teaching the same subject. Those teachers who were asked to talk at conferences benefited from the experience, which no doubt required them to reflect on the practice they were describing. The relevance of subject differences at the secondary level was also reported by Hodgen and Marshall (2005) in the KMOFAP project.

The funds made available for schools to support the implementation of the programme were widely acknowledged by teachers as central to supporting change in practice. Head teachers had freedom in the deployment of these funds. One reported using funds to release teachers for a scheme she described as 'blind dating', in which teachers were randomly paired to observe each other's teaching and then spend time together in a relaxed atmosphere to discuss their views. This underlines the importance of human resources as of foremost importance in professional learning.

## Wales

The arrangements that replaced national tests were designed to provide support for teachers' own assessment and to encourage confidence of teachers in others' judgements. An important part of this is to help teachers understand the meaning of standards and to realize what is actually being required.

The arrangements at Key Stage 2 place emphasis on supporting and securing teacher assessment via moderation meetings for groups of teachers. Guidance for school clusters has been produced in the form of a guidance document (DCELLS, 2008f) which was distributed to schools in January 2008. This draws on practice identified by schools and local education authorities, and pays regard to the development of the statutory primary/secondary transition arrangements implemented from September 2008. At Key Stage 3, the aim is to strengthen the end-of-key stage assessment by verification of school-based systems and procedures and by external moderation of sample evidence of the teachers' understanding and application of the national curriculum level descriptions. The quality of teacher assessment will then be recognized by awarding schools 'accredited centre status'. These moderation activities are a form of professional learning, allowing teachers to share examples of students' work, to justify their assessment of it and to align their judgements. As found elsewhere, some subject differences emerged, English teachers being more willing than mathematics and science teachers to give up tests.

## Northern Ireland

Following a pilot study from 2004 to 2006, materials were developed and made available on the Internet to support trainers, senior management and teachers in developing AfL. These materials included booklets of guidance for primary and secondary schools, explaining AfL and introducing practical strategies. For professional learning providers there were training units in the form of PowerPoint presentations on such topics as 'Sharing Learning Intentions and Success Criteria', 'Formative Feedback', 'Effective Questioning' and 'Helping Children to Reflect on Their Learning'.

The Council for Curriculum, Examinations and Assessment (CCEA), described the pilot project as 'action research' meaning that teachers were encouraged 'to experiment with aspects of the methodology of assessment for learning' and to 'adapt the theory and principles of formative assessment to suit their own teaching context and their individual pupils' (CCEA, 2006: 6). However, the extent to which the teachers developed ownership over the methods they used is unclear. Shirley Clarke's approaches to formative assessment were presented at an early stage, both through live presentation and through the provision of her books (Clarke, 2003). When asked to choose from the AfL strategies, it is therefore not surprising that almost 80 per cent of teachers chose to begin by adopting 'learning intentions and success criteria' producing a rash of WALT ('We Are Learning To') boards. The bulk of the remaining 20 per cent began with 'questioning techniques'. This left 'feedback' and 'peer- and self-assessment' to be tackled later.

Reports from the pilot, gathered via a survey questionnaire sent to all participants, indicated that the strategies to which they were introduced were completely new to the teachers. Despite being described as 'action research', it was clear that the approach was to present the key strategies for teachers to try out (model C, trial and adjustment). Given that summative assessment has largely dominated education in Northern Ireland, the changes that were found after only a short time were very positive. Pupils were described as being more confident, persevering, with raised self-esteem, knowing what they had to do and showing a better use of language. Teachers were more focused on the needs of pupils, were planning for formative assessment, were more reflective about their practice and had changed their pedagogy.

However, some survey results showed a considerable gap between intentions and the short-term changes after one or two years. Over 30 per cent of respondents did not think that the project benefited all pupils, or that pupils' behaviour had improved as a result of the project. The same proportion reported that pupils were not identifying the next steps in their own learning. There was particular concern (over 82 per cent) that parents had not been informed about the project and that they were not able to contribute to the assessment of their children. A number of findings point to the institutional support that is needed when teachers undertake to make changes in practice. Relevant school policies need to be changed and time built in to teachers' schedules for planning. All members of the school staff need to know about the project, even if they are not involved directly in making changes, making the case for school management as a focus for professional learning. As reported in other projects, teachers sharing experiences with other teachers was of considerable help. The plea to 'not try to do everything so quickly' underlines the need to allow time for planning, sharing and reflection.

## England

Two projects, funded by the Department for Education and Skills (DfES), were developed by the Qualifications and Curriculum Authority, QCA, and the National Strategies (DCSF, 2009d) to help teachers' assessment: 'assessing pupils' progress Key Stage 3' and 'monitoring children's progress Key Stage 2' (QCA, 2007b). The Key Stage 3 project, which was subject to an evaluation of its 2003/5 pilot (QCA, 2006b), has been completed and the materials published on the Key Stage 3 Strategy website. These materials aim to help teachers make judgements of the levels at which their pupils are working in reading, writing and mathematics. At Key Stage 3 they comprise guidance on periodically making a 'best fit' judgement of pupils' work, usually once a term. The guidance is based on the use of 'assessment focuses', which unpick level descriptions of the national curriculum into a series of criteria relating to key aspects of the attainment target at each level. A handbook gives some examples of work to illustrate the standard of work at each level. There are also banks of tasks for teachers to use with individual pupils or the whole class as part of normal work to supplement the information available about particular pupils or parts of the curriculum.

The published materials for Key Stage 3 are reported as contributing to improved learning and more responsive teaching. The evidence for this comes from teachers' use of the ongoing summative assessment to indicate how they might adjust their programmes through identifying the needs of individual pupils or groups or the gaps in evidence they can gather. Training for teachers was provided during the development and trial of materials. For the Key Stage 3 materials, two teachers from each participating trial school attended training sessions and two summer conferences. According to the QCA:

> Guidance was provided...for teachers on how to identify suitable examples of independent work for assessment and on the application of assessment criteria to pupils' on-going work. Teachers were supplied with annotated samples of collections of work to support their understanding of standards.
>
> (QCA, 2006b: 12)

The training was spread over the year:

> In the autumn term the...underpinning rationale was explained and standards were exemplified. Teachers were introduced to the use of the tasks and the data collection requirements. In the spring term a package of materials was sent out to local authorities' consultants for use with their project teachers in preparation for the next round of assessment. A majority followed the advice to hold a meeting to go over materials and arrangements with their teachers, while others visited individual schools. Towards the end of the summer term, conferences were held to present some general interim findings, and to provide an opportunity for teachers to share reflections on their experiences.
>
> (QCA, 2006b: 13)

Although explanation of the 'underpinning rationale' is mentioned as being included in the materials, the training does seem to have inclined towards model D, practice of techniques, rather than anything more 'bottom-up'. Among the challenges identified in the training of teachers and phasing of implementation were the existing policies of schools where there is over-reliance on tests and the need for the understanding and support of senior management, underlining their importance as focuses for professional learning to ensure maximum impact.

## Lessons from the examples

### Formative and summative – or just good assessment?

Two of the issues raised earlier refer to the relationship between assessment for formative and summative purposes. Whether a project began as essentially concerned with the formative use of assessment (as in KMOFAP) or the summative use (as in KOSAP and the Birmingham/Oxfordshire project) there was evidence of teachers using the same assessment data for formative and summative uses. It appears that while a theoretical distinction can be made, in practice summative and formative assessment are so closely involved in teachers' day-to-day work that separation may not be helpful.

However, it is important for teachers to realize that there are different purposes and that to serve these purposes, the assessment has to meet certain criteria. For instance, using summative assessment results for formative use does not require the close attention to reliability that a purely summative use requires. On the other hand, allowing the formative use to detract from the rigour that summative assessment requires would be to endanger confidence in teachers' judgements. Professional learning courses therefore need to make more explicit the different *uses* of the same evidence and help teachers to ensure that their assessment meets the requirements of these uses – whether formative or summative – most effectively.

The mixture of project focuses, some on developing formative assessment and some on developing summative assessment by teachers, raises the question of whether the professional learning approach differs, or ought to differ, according to the focus. Teachers' assessment is something that teachers already do, whether to meet statutory requirements or for reporting to parents, carers and other teachers and for school records. By contrast formative assessment, while being widely encouraged, is not a requirement or, as yet, extensively practised. It could be argued, then, that to improve teachers' summative assessment, all that is necessary is to have the experience of just doing things differently. Indeed, in the summative assessment projects above a good deal of time was spent in studying pupils' work. Nevertheless, there are important reasons for using teachers' assessment as opposed to tests, which teachers need to understand. These relate to validity, making it possible to include all that is taught in what is assessed, but also to reliability (see Chapter 2). The reliability of teachers' judgements can be made comparable with that of tests if appropriate training and moderation steps are taken, which is the reason for professional learning focusing on the use of criteria and procedures for moderation of the judgements.

### Starting from principles or practice?

One of the dilemmas for professional learning providers, emerging from the consideration of the projects examined under the auspices of the ARIA study, concerns the role of principles and theory in helping teachers to change their practices. In several of the projects, the professional learning leaders recognized that teachers, rather than beginning with a consideration of why change is necessary, want to start from knowing how to implement new assessment procedures and to know what techniques are likely to work. However, it is also evident that unless reasons for change are understood, techniques are likely to be followed somewhat blindly; they will not be adapted as necessary for different situations and will eventually become less helpful. It may well be that, as in the case of the KMOFAP teachers, interest in knowing about why and how new practices work develops only after seeing that they *do* work. Underlying theory is probably best introduced to develop understanding of practice rather than as a starting point. One way or another, teachers need to have a reason for changing existing practices and adopting new ones.

## 'Bottom-up' or 'top-down'?

A second, related, dilemma concerns the approach – the 'bottom-up' or 'top-down' dimension. In essence, bottom-up starts from questions, while top-down begins by providing answers. Although the former is more likely to lead to ownership and commitment to change, time and feasibility come into decisions about whether it is practicable. Teachers involved in model A and B type activities (full or simulated participation) value the experience of finding answers for themselves and recognize how it contributes to their professional learning. But making this kind of experience available to all teachers is clearly not feasible and some formality and uniformity of experience becomes inevitable when the aim is to make changes at a national level. The structure required for large-scale dissemination may make model D type courses (practice of techniques) seem inevitable, particularly when they are part of a cascade model of dissemination (see Chapter 5). However, 'training' materials can have within them the potential, even the requirement, for teachers to have the experiences that lead them to relate what they learn to their own context. In other words, the materials can provide them with options to try out and develop, more as in model C, possibly leading to the simulated participation of model B.

## The need for discussion and reflection

Teachers recognize that they need time to reflect and to incorporate new practices into their teaching and are likely to resent being 'done to', as noted in the evaluation of the formative assessment project in Jersey. They also find it helpful to spend some of this time talking to others and sharing experiences. Those teachers who experienced model A, full participation, whether for formative assessment as in KMOFAP or summative assessment as in the Birmingham/Oxfordshire project, found this more useful than being given materials. But those who cannot have model A opportunities from the start, and have to depend initially on materials, nevertheless ought to have the opportunity to meet with others and reflect on their own and each other's efforts to change practice. The interaction among teachers enables those who are having more difficulty to learn from the success of others, acting to counter the 'dilution' of the message that is inherent in any cascade dissemination model. This suggests that some of the resources for professional learning should be reserved for ensuring that this interaction can take place.

The evidence used in teachers' assessment of students need not be restricted to written work and indeed ought not to be if assessment is to go beyond the basic skills and knowledge. The equipment to video pupils is widely available and can be used by pupils as well as teachers, giving evidence of self- and peer-assessment as well as their grasp of content in deciding what to record. Regardless of the medium used to present evidence, professional learning experiences ought to give opportunity for reflection on and, if necessary, reformulation of the criteria being used and the use made of the results. There is just as much commitment needed for good summative assessment by teachers as there is for implementing formative assessment. While the aims and content of the professional learning are different for these two purposes, those who identify for themselves what needs to be done are more likely to understand the principles and to be able to self-assess their progress towards the aims of making reliable judgements in the case of summative assessment, and of helping next steps in the case of formative assessment.

### Feedback for teachers

When teachers begin to make changes and enter what may be, for them, uncharted waters, they need some feedback that can tell whether they are navigating successfully. This can come either from their own observation of the effects of their actions; for example, responses of pupils that show that their actions are worthwhile and helpful to their engagement in learning. Or it may come from professional learning developers who formatively assess teachers' progress in the way that the teachers are encouraged to do in using assessment to support their pupils' learning. This argues against having an overly unstructured bottom-up approach. As well as questions and problems, the teachers need to know what they are aiming for.

### Catering for different starting points

The examples of projects examined in the ARIA study also show that it is important for professional learning to start from the initial understanding of teachers, just as teachers should find out and start teaching from where pupils are. The experience of KOSAP showed that even with experienced teachers, there still can be misunderstandings of the differences and similarities between formative and summative assessment or, indeed, the meaning of assessment. Not all teachers will follow the same route in developing understanding and changing assessment practice and differences are to be expected. Some dimensions of progression in implementing changes were identified at the start of this chapter. Another, particularly relevant to change in assessment, is in terms of teachers beginning as 'novices' in the implementation of new procedures or materials and then becoming more 'competent' and eventually 'expert'. The characteristic differences between the novice and the expert across different fields of activity are described by Bransford et al. (1999) primarily in terms of the ability to see patterns and to identify the principles that apply. In the case of teachers, experts have a clear idea of how to help students learn and consistently use appropriate strategies based on the information they constantly gather about their students' learning. Novices, on the other hand, are concerned with the specific techniques rather than the big picture and with their own role rather than that of their students. 'Competent' teachers have progressed beyond novice status but not reached that of expert. They are more independent in choosing teaching strategies and more aware of how their students respond than novices but have not acquired the overview of teaching and learning of experts. The development of teachers from novice to expert is not necessarily a function of experience or years as a teacher. When new demands are made, all teachers are likely to begin as novices and progress at different rates towards competence and expertise.

## Conclusion

Research, for example Hattie (2003), has pointed to the teacher as the single most important factor affecting student achievement, so professional learning has a key part to play in the process of any change in education. Despite this, hard evidence of the impact on students' learning is difficult to obtain, due to the long chain of events between the initial input for the teachers and their students' learning. However potentially effective the professional learning experience may be, a teacher may not engage fully with, or may misunderstand, some of the intended messages. Even when teachers fully understand the techniques and reasons for any new practice, they may be restricted in implementing the necessary changes by school, local or national policies and by the expectations of those involved as users of assessment, such as parents, employers and higher education.

It follows that if changes are to be made, school management, local authorities and policy makers need to understand the rationale for changes, what they involve and what support the teachers need. This has been underlined in almost every case discussed, particularly when change at national level is the aim.

Thus, those providing professional learning must recognize that teachers are not necessarily free to change their assessment practices, even if they so wish. The realities of the context of teachers' work may, for example, require that students are given tests and these realities need to be taken into account in helping teachers to improve their assessment practice. The practices of other teachers in the school and pressure from parents may conflict with what is required for formative assessment, such as non-judgemental feedback. In addition, there are the effects of the teachers' own backgrounds, experiences and beliefs, which will transform, perhaps unconsciously, the messages intended to be conveyed. Consequently, there are too many variables influencing students' learning for this to be a useful measure of the effectiveness of teachers' professional learning. More useful is the qualitative information that has been reported in the studies discussed here. Hasty evaluation of professional learning on the basis of students' learning must be avoided.

Key features relating to professional learning drawn from the projects examined in the ARIA study include the need for:

- a structure of professional learning combining concentrated inputs with follow-up discussion to enable teachers to try out new techniques, then report and review;
- encouragement for teachers to go beyond using techniques and to understand principles so that they can adapt and develop procedures to suit their working context;
- inclusion of head teachers and school management in professional learning about new approaches to assessment;
- time for teachers and others to reflect on new procedures;
- access to the experience of other teachers with whom they can identify;
- flexibility in provision to take account of teachers' different starting points and rates of progress;
- funding and other evidence of official support for making changes;
- clarity about the goals of the professional learning;
- opportunities for feedback on progress, through discussion and self-evaluation;
- a variety of different forms of input and professional learning experience with sufficient time overall for change to become well established.

## Questions for reflection

1. In what circumstances might each of the models of professional learning be most appropriate?

2. What are the main points to be considered in deciding an approach to professional learning for developing practice in assessment for learning?

3. What differences, if any, would there be if the assessment were for a mainly summative purpose?

## Note

1. Shirley Clarke is an educational consultant who has made considerable impact in schools across the UK through her professional development workshops and books (Clarke, 2003).

# 7 Teachers as self-agents of change

*John Gardner*

Agency, in the sense of 'agent of change', is a key concept and process that needs to be thoroughly understood if effective and sustained change in assessment practice is to be established. A variety of dimensions of agency come under the umbrella terms, bottom-up and top-down (dealt with comprehensively in the preceding two chapters). This chapter considers different types of agency but extends the bottom-up notion specifically into how teachers themselves are imperative to the successful development of teacher assessment in any school. Importantly, any expression of self-agency should be assured of external support whether outside the classroom and within the school, or external to the school. The chapter also emphasizes the importance of self-agency in creating a school culture of readiness to consider and embrace change where appropriate.

## Introduction

The concept of 'agent of change' came into regular usage in the education community following Fullan's *Change Forces* book, published in 1993. In this brief but widely read work, he popularized notions of change that made sense to a broad range of educationalists including teachers and researchers. Drawing on existing practice and research, he made snappy generalizations, which had the ring of experiential truth about them. To quote just a few, his lessons from the 'new paradigm of change' (1993: 21) enabled him to claim that 'Neither centralization nor decentralization works' when it comes to the pursuit of sustained change; that 'Connection with the wider environment is critical for success' in ensuring change does not become isolated and avails of all possible support; and finally that 'Every person is a change agent'. Inevitably any discussion of educational change will rehearse these and other generalizations. However, as a central theme in the pursuit of change in assessment practice, the work of the ARIA study suggests that the concept and operational dimensions of agency need to be thoroughly understood if optimal conditions for appropriate, effective and sustained change in assessment practice are to be established.

## Conceptions of agency

There are two common understandings of the term 'agent': someone who is an advocate and promotes the interests of another person or organization, or someone who goes further than this and undertakes actions on behalf of another person or organization. These two senses of an agent of change can be broadened in education to include agents that are not people; for example, peer pressure, public opinion and professional learning, which are perhaps better described as processes.

What is common to any form of agent, however, is the role that it plays as an intermediary between the status quo and a proposed new approach. In education, for example, the target may be an established practice or method, upon which someone or something is acting to change. In the present context, change agents might be said to be operating at the interface between external and teacher assessment in schools. While there may be significant differences in the extent to which school systems engage with teacher assessment, with it being noticeably less integrated in the school system in England than in the systems in Northern Ireland, Wales and Scotland, the direction of change across the UK is towards more teacher assessment (see Chapter 3).

There are some notable agents that could compete for the title of 'most significant' in this process, such as the growth in professional recognition that assessment, as far as possible, should contribute to learning; that is, it should have a formative influence. With external summative assessments (e.g. GCSEs) rarely used in this manner, the trend is partly explained by the fact that teacher assessment is held to be much more amenable to formative usage. Other front-runner agents might include the growing awareness that too much testing may have a counterproductive effect on learning outcomes for many students, or that testing for purposes other than individual outcomes is arguably a gross misuse of assessment. Prime among these latter purposes is 'accountability', in which assessments of individual students' performance are used primarily to appraise teacher and school performance. There are many other candidates for agency, varying from the demonstrable but not widely appreciated extent of unreliability in external test scores to the equally demonstrable and more widely appreciated value of appropriate feedback in support of learning.

Unpacking how a system changes, therefore, is not a simple process and depends crucially on how well chosen the change agents are.

Approaching the issue from a different direction, it is worth exploring what or who might be the textbook change agents in education systems. The list is fairly succinct: teachers, school management/managers and local authority personnel might dominate the 'people' variant of agency while government policy and new knowledge (from research, etc.) might form the vanguard of the 'process' variant. Viewing the process of change from this perspective introduces another facet of agency. If the agent of change is different from the operational subject of the change, there is the likelihood that it is a 'top-down'-driven model of change.

## Top-down, bottom-up or something in between?

Approaches to professional development and learning have been set out comprehensively in Chapter 6 and this section focuses more on the agency of the desired changes than the model of professional development. Changing classroom practice by policy decree (e.g. subject to regulation and subsequent monitoring) or by the 'supported pressure' of professional development programmes and appropriate resource provision, would describe top-down approaches normally associated with a centralized agency. Sometimes these can be very effective. For example, school development planning was originally a mandated change in the mid-1990s but is now a firmly embedded process in the vast majority of schools. Any grumbles about imposition are far outweighed by the recognition of the benefits to be gained. On the other hand, repeated attempts to kick start information and communications technology (ICT) integration in classroom practice, through major funding of training, have had a much more patchy and, in some notable instances, ineffectual impact. A particularly well-researched UK-wide programme, the NOF (New Opportunities Fund), sponsored programme for teachers, has attracted criticism arising from evaluations by Preston (2004) and OFSTED (2002) for England and Wales, Galanouli et al. (2004) for Northern Ireland, and Conlon (2004) and Kirkwood et al. (2000) for Scotland.

The other traditional perspective on change agency is 'bottom-up'. In this mode the change is promoted and brought to action by those who give it its operational focus. If classroom practice is the change context, then the most obvious bottom-up agent is the classroom teacher. Generally speaking, change in such circumstances will arise as a result of some specific stimulus such as peer dialogue or personal research and reading. There are circumstances too in which students can act as the bottom-up change agent. These include the process known as 'pester power'; the students know and appreciate what one teacher does and they lobby another teacher to adopt the same approach. The student bottom-up process may also be initiated as a result of being asked (pupil consultation, pupil voice) about any improvements in their classroom experience that they feel could be made.

Another feature of the top-down versus bottom-up analysis revolves around the theory versus practice debate (see Chapter 6). Should an external agent provide the teachers with a practical introduction to an innovative, or at least new to them, classroom process? Arguably, this allows the teachers to see the desirable change in action before trying it out themselves. A deeper understanding through reflection and consideration of the theory and literature may then be attended to later. A counter-view might be that there should be an introduction to the concepts that form the change focus, along with the research and reports from schools that provide evidence of its efficacy, before the teachers try it out for themselves. In the former possibility the external agent could be the teacher in the next classroom (a type of peer agency, more 'sideways' than specifically top-down) or in both cases it could be the promotion of professional learning through exposure to professional development activities provided by a local authority (more explicitly top-down).

In this debate about which should come first, the theory or the practice, there are shades of what Sfard (1998) has called the acquisition versus participation metaphors of learning. Applied to professional learning, the distinction implies a choice between designing participative practical experiences prior to promoting reflection and deeper assimilation of the principles, theories and concepts, and an acquisition design in which the teachers are relatively passive and in extreme cases are told what to do, perhaps through regulation or policy demands but certainly in a top-down form. The research literature offers no dependable conclusions on the debate as to which is better. And in a large majority of the initiatives studied in ARIA, the process was considerably more organic than either of these restricted approaches, with circumstance and opportunity determining the blending of the different issues and approaches.

## Self-agency as a key to change

An alternative to the choice of theory first or practice-first arises from self-reflection or individual professional learning in which teachers act as their own agency of change, a variant of bottom-up. This might come about through 'picking up' relevant ideas from professional dialogue or from reading the professional and academic literature on the potential benefits of the proposed changes. They then either seek support or have a go themselves. In the latter case, the self-agency is unambiguous; the teachers themselves derive the impetus for change from their own professional reading, reflection and collegial interaction. Self-agency is a powerful device in fostering change because it draws on self-motivation. It may arise in the manner just mentioned (self-reflection, reading, etc.) or it might be 'sparked off' by charismatic colleagues or initiatives sponsored by either local authorities or central government acting as awareness-raising agents. What appears strongly to be the case throughout the projects examined under the auspices of the ARIA study (see Chapter 6) is that unless teachers are committed through self-agency to any particular change, the prospects for successful dissemination and professional learning, leading to its sustained practice, are likely to be slim.

What has also been obvious from the ARIA work is that agency, while requiring a considerable degree of initial and ongoing self-agency, also requires external dimensions of support. Support conventionally ranges from awareness-raising, in the form of information and advice, to direct interventions including professional development events, which themselves are supported by appropriate resources and funding such as time out of school. The varieties of support in between include school-based staff development, peer support and whole school development planning processes.

## Awareness and 'hearts and minds' as elements of readiness

Looking at agency from a teacher-as-learner perspective; that is, with a focus directly on teachers as primary agents in sponsoring and assimilating changes in their own practice, it is reasonable to apply some of the principles we know about learners and their motivation. Paraphrasing Black et al. (2003: 78), planners need to begin any change process by carefully locating the teachers' base position. A self-administered analysis of needs suggests itself as the sensible way forward, to ensure change conditions are as tailored as possible to the individual. However, no needs analysis, whether by the teachers for themselves or by others for the teachers, could hope to be effective or purposeful if the teachers are not sufficiently aware of the change issues and their potential. Common sense would identify some degree of readiness to be influenced as preferable to a cold-calling sales approach with no prior warning or preparation.

In the majority of initiatives aiming at change in assessment, awareness-raising forms a major part of the initial stages. The outcomes of prior research will often provide the rationale and act as a form of agency in promoting change. There seems little doubt, for example, that

Black and Wiliam's timely review (1998a) of the educational potential of appropriate formative (classroom) assessment lit the touch paper of radical reflection on the role of assessment in pedagogy and learning. Other major publications had made similar claims some years before (e.g. Crooks, 1988; Sadler, 1989), though arguably on less robust bases. However, the prevailing circumstances of ever more testing, league tables and top-down educational ideologies provided a fertile environment for Black and Wiliam's ideas to find an audience, prompting the rapid growth of interest and engagement by the teaching community in an alternative paradigm of assessment.

The effect may be likened to credible research providing teachers with room to manoeuvre beyond the confines of their established practice, a warrant for them to experiment and try out new approaches. Awareness of the potential for improved student motivation and attainment has spread like wildfire over the period since Black and Wiliam's (1998a) publication, and has enabled several national initiatives to be undertaken in assessment policy and practice. Examples include the assessment is for learning (AiFL) programme in Scotland and the Northern Ireland Revised Curriculum with its integrated assessment for learning policy (see Chapter 3).

Holmes et al. (2007) have placed the need for good awareness of the potential benefits firmly at the base of any professional learning development (see Figure 7.1). Simply put, teachers must know and understand the context and purpose of change sufficiently to evaluate their own needs

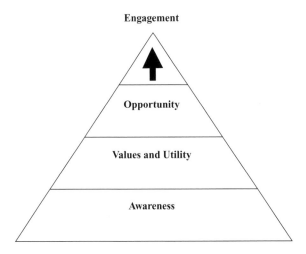

**Figure 7.1** The foundational importance of awareness for initiating professional learning (reproduced with permission from Holmes et al., 2007)

and hopefully to develop the desire to adopt the proposed change. The model then moves through stages in which the teachers' values and the perceived utility of the change converge and are in sympathy with adopting it. The necessary opportunities for professional learning and practice to be grasped as teachers move to full engagement.

It seems almost trite to observe that the prospect of effective change will be considerably disadvantaged if it comes completely 'out of the blue'. Regardless of how the change situation might proceed, this model therefore argues that the initiating agent must be an awareness of the change context. But how do we characterize the stage between knowing about something (awareness) and preparing to do something about it (seeking or grasping the opportunity)?

In the Holmes et al. (2007) diagram (see Figure 7.1), the next stage of the building of readiness to learn and change is 'values and utility'. Awareness-raising alone would quickly founder if in fact the teachers concerned are not particularly supportive of the changes being proposed; if they see no benefit or value for themselves or if they cannot envisage any utility in supporting their teaching. Such circumstances can create substantial counter-agency influences.

For example, following on a process of awareness-raising, some teachers may develop educational or even philosophical objections to the proposed changes and some may also manifest a degree of antipathy towards them, perhaps arising from a variety of not uncommon perspectives or conditions. In the projects studied through ARIA, these have included workload concerns ('change means more work'), insufficient knowledge or understanding of the change process and its intentions, or an uncertainty about whether the changes will bring benefits to them or their students. Where change demands new skills, the problems associated with confidence, competence and time to develop the skills can all conspire to act as counter-agencies. Professional 'face' can also be a countervailing force if the perception of a deficit in skills – 'I have a need' or perhaps worse: 'They [policy makers, the Inspectorate etc] think I have a need' – is made a feature of the justification for change.

Awareness-raising alone will also founder if there is no attempt made to bring the teachers on board. Arguably, what seems to be as important as awareness in being an early element in the plan of a change process, is that the teachers should be positively disposed to learning something new and to undertaking personal development in it. This 'hearts and minds' predisposition, a willingness and readiness to reflect on one's own practice, to learn and to change it, is probably key to the success of any change and may therefore constitute a general rather than a specific condition. It is not difficult to conceive of teachers who are resistant to change *per se*; that is, the nature of the change has no bearing on their negative reaction.

If these teachers represent anything other than a small proportion of the community being exposed to a change, the change itself could be seriously confounded.

Generally speaking there is an argument that says we should collectively aim to create a culture of professional reflection and pursuit of improvement that can sustain continuous improvement and changed practice. However, for specific change contexts, there needs to be a well-formed plan of action to develop a positive disposition to the change in question. This means the convergence of the teachers' values with a recognition of the utility of the change to produce a strong self-agency, which then drives the process on to the third level of Figure 7.1 in which opportunities for change are grasped.

## Counter-productive agency

In the absence of strong espousal (hearts and minds), several conditions and processes can amount in their effect to counter-productive agency in a change context.

For example, the requirement for compliance with a top-down policy, whether within a school or from an external body, may lead to a down-grading of the perceived value of the practice that forms the focus of the change. An example might be a senior management team (SMT) requirement that every teacher should begin each lesson with a WALT (We Are Learning To) board. Though intended to be the outcome of a teacher and a class sharing learning objectives, it may quickly become a must-do that is presented to the class with the minimum of discourse. Even worse, it may merely tick a box when a member of the senior management team calls to monitor its usage. When the compliance monitoring fades, this minimal engagement will also tend to become erratic until it fades away completely.

Indifference is a condition that also has the potential for counter-productive agency. If a change is adopted simply because it is relatively easy to adopt and is not perceived as a particularly useful activity, it has little prospect of being sustained. It may be the case that good experience arising from indifferent motives can ultimately stimulate a more positive espousal but it is more likely a doomed endeavour.

Unilateralism is a process that can promote both productive and counterproductive agency. The enthusiasm of the lone innovator can inspire some colleagues or repel others. Similarly, top-down diktats, whether from school managers or external authorities, will almost always fuel resentment, especially if the changes are perceived to be under-resourced or to encroach on professional judgement or personal time.

## Conclusion

Self-agency is a powerful element in ensuring the success of teacher assessment in schools. If teachers have the evidence that teacher assessment will improve their pupils' learning, and that there will be consequent benefits for themselves and their teaching, they will respond positively. Schools and others wishing to develop teacher assessment must strive to cultivate and capture this self-agency if the changes are to be assimilated into sustainable practice.

---

### Questions for reflection

1. In introducing an innovation in assessment
   a. What approaches might be adopted to promote purposeful and effective agency among teachers?
   b. What possible implications might there be to promote agency amongst learners?
   c. In what ways might agency be an issue for other groups; for example, policy makers, parents?

2. Reflecting on a recent innovation, to what extent was the importance of agency built into the design of the innovation? What strategies were used in practice?

---

# Part III

# Keeping it going

# 8 Making a difference: evaluating the impact of innovations in assessment

*Gordon Stobart*

An innovation seeks to make a difference, so something should change. How do we go about evaluating such change? This chapter considers what may be involved in assessing the impact of classroom initiatives. Many innovations have come through professional development initiatives that place more emphasis on teachers' personal responses than on systematic collection of data. This chapter looks for ways of providing evidence that can provide more systematic and widely accepted support for the claims made. These include baseline information that provides information about the situation at the start of the innovation that can then be compared with information available after implementation. The claims being made for the initiative may range from a specific aspect of assessment to broader aspirations; for example, to improve classroom learning. The broader the claim, the more complex it is to establish whether change took place. Different forms of evidence are considered along with their potential limitations. Ways of incorporating impact measures into assessment initiatives are also examined.

## Introduction

An innovation seeks to do something new and if it is successful we would expect to see differences. What kind of difference will depend on what was intended and what was possible. The reason for an assessment initiative may be specific; for example, improving the consistency of marking in primary English. Determining whether marking has become more consistent may be relatively straightforward if we can compare levels of agreement before and after the initiative, or if we ask teachers about how they are marking pupils' work now and whether this is more consistent than their previous practice. However, the broader the scope of the innovation and the more complex the aims, the more difficult it may be to establish what the impact has been.

This is particularly the case if the innovation is just one of several initiatives in which a school is involved or if other major policy changes are also being implemented in schools. How do we tell which changes are a consequence of the innovation. What are the results of other changes and what may be the product of interactions between them? For example, if an innovative programme of assessment for learning (AfL) was introduced at the same time as the government's revised primary strategy, with its curriculum and teaching advice, how do we determine what caused any observed changes?

If the goal is couched in broad terms; for example, 'better learning', this may lead to differing expectations of what this means. For policy makers and school managers 'better learning' may be understood as 'better performance' in terms of national curriculum levels and examination grades. Any initiative which claims to improve learning would be expected to lead to improved results, since many policy makers will equate learning with test performance. Improved learning would then be recognized through improved grades, a claim that has been contested by others (see Tymms, 2004).

For most of those involved in the initiatives reviewed in the ARIA project, 'better learning' was seen in broader terms – it was about changed attitudes, better understanding and more learner autonomy. So the impact may be in terms of changes to the classroom climate, different ways of teaching and improved attitudes to learning rather than directly on results. Even within a broadly defined 'better learning', this still leaves the question of what we might expect in terms of academic outcomes, since improved learning might reasonably be expected to lead, at some point, to improved test or examination results. Harlen and James (1997) have argued that an exception to this claim would arise if the quality of the summative assessment is so poor that it does not tap into the kind of deep learning that has been encouraged and so benefits those prepared through rote and surface learning. This was not a case made by any of the projects examined under ARIA, so for most of them there was the assumption there should be some direct and positive impact on assessment results.

## How is the impact of an innovation in assessment to be evaluated?

The innovations we reviewed were concerned with complex learning processes and attitudes that did not lend themselves to simple measures.

James and Brown faced the same question in their review of *learning outcomes* of the projects funded by the Economic and Social Research Council's Teaching and Learning Research Programme (TLRP). They questioned the emphasis on:

> ... performance and bureaucratic models of learning which focus on measurable skills and attainment targets. What is clear, not least through the work of this programme is that the limitations of such perspectives constrain thinking about, and divert attention from, other valuable forms of learning. Furthermore, their requirements of objective, quantitative measurement techniques for assessment divert attention from the consideration of broader issues such as how to make judgements about process learning, long-term retention of learning, unintended learning outcomes and self-assessment of learning.
>
> (James and Brown, 2005: 8)

This left them with the problem of how to demonstrate whether or not the research interventions they had funded had made the intended differences in learning. Their review of school-based projects generated seven categories of outcomes:

1. *attainments* – based on conventional measures of knowledge, skills, and so on;
2. *understanding* – of ideas, concepts, processes;
3. *cognitive and creative* – creating 'new' knowledge by learners;
4. *using* – how to develop and apply practical and technological skills in appropriate contexts;
5. *higher-order learning* – advanced thinking, reasoning, metacognition that transcend other learning outcomes – 'agreement about how they are to be assessed is even more difficult to achieve';
6. *dispositions* – attitudes; perceptions motivations necessary if learners are inclined to learn effectively in the context where learning takes place;
7. *membership, inclusion, self-worth* – readiness to participate in contributions to the group where the learning takes place. (p 11)

The TLRP review also commented that those who submitted proposals focused on 'ideas and approaches to teaching that they confidently believed would improve learning. They were much less confident, however, about how they would go about demonstrating whether or not their interventions had made the intended differences to learning' (James and Brown, 2005: 8). This has a number of parallels with the initiatives reviewed as part of the ARIA project.

## Capturing change

The TLRP categories may provide a useful framework for looking at the projects that the ARIA study reviewed. Their main limitation is that many of the projects had multiple goals, for which the outcomes were only formulated in very general and often aspirational terms. This raises the question of how to determine the quality of the evidence on which claims were based and whether the broad aims had been met with the desired impact.

For instance, most of the projects reported improvements in terms of changes to teachers' understanding (James and Brown's category 2), practices (category 4) and pupils' attitudes (category 6). The evidence to support these claims in most evaluations was based on teacher perceptions of changes in their own practices and their pupils' attitudes and behaviour. Because these innovations were treated as part of teachers' professional development, rather than as research projects, there was generally little imperative to collect information systematically about what had changed. This often led to assertions that a particular approach had worked, based on the teachers' informal observations. While this is a legitimate source of evidence, it limits the generation of more general conclusions if no further supporting evidence is provided. To use the TLRP term, the question then to be asked is: Can such claims be *warranted*?

The use of *teacher perceptions* was the dominant form of evidence in the projects reviewed by ARIA. This generally took the form of data from either questionnaires or interviews. Many of the larger and more research-based projects were independently evaluated and did encourage checking of these claims against other data. The evaluations often sought forms of *triangulation* that used several lines of evidence to see if they supported each other. For example, teachers' claims could then be supported or challenged by using pupils' attitudes or their views about what difference the innovation had made. A more complex form of triangulation is to assess whether an innovation has led to improved achievement (see below). This may always be problematical, since so much else is going on in schools that it would be hard to attribute change, or lack of change, to any single cause.

The emphasis on triangulation of evidence stems from the recognition that there will invariably be no 'killer proof' of a programme working, a single form of evidence that can be presented as incontrovertible ('the smoking gun'). Instead, we will generally be looking for multiple weak lines of evidence that point in the same direction. If they do we may place some confidence in our account that the innovation has had an impact – though this is always open to the challenge of alternative interpretations of the findings. An enduring alternative explanation is that of the Hawthorne Effect[1] (Schwartzman, 1993), in which the impact comes not from what is being done but from the fact that the participants are being studied and they respond positively to this.

What emerges from the project reports is a strong sense of *teacher belief* that the formative assessment innovations had benefited both teaching and learning. Stobart and Stoll (2005) have argued this 'it worked' approach is a powerful source of evidence for teachers and policy makers, who may otherwise place less significance on less accessible and immediate research findings. There is therefore a tension between the 'it worked' evidence having an immediate appeal for those directly involved but perhaps not providing sufficient evidence to convince those who are less directly involved. Nevertheless, teacher advocacy is acknowledged to be one of the most powerful forms of dissemination of classroom innovation. The impact of any innovation is often communicated through the enthusiasm of the teachers who are describing it. Third parties, such as policy makers and researchers, share the occupational hazard that we tend to want more systematic information about what has happened and how it might be explained.

It is important, therefore, to look at some of the methods available for gauging the impact of an innovation. Drawing on a wider literature, it is possible to provide some examples of research designs that go beyond informal observation by teachers of the impact of their changed classroom practices and their pupils' responses.

## A framework for evaluating impact

One of the tenets of AfL, which was the focus of the majority of the projects considered in the ARIA study, is to establish 'where learners are in their learning' and 'where they need to get to'. This can be extended to the evaluation of the impact of such projects, along with those that sought to develop teachers' summative assessments. A framework would include:

1. baseline descriptors of pre-innovation practices and standards;
2. statements of intended outcomes;
3. evidence of outcomes;
4. unintended consequences;
5. interpretations including alternative explanations.

By focusing on the initiatives considered by the ARIA study, these headings can be elaborated into a more detailed series of questions. This is not intended as a checklist since some questions will only apply to particular forms of innovation.

### 1 Baseline descriptors of pre-innovation practices and standards

This section raises issues about the extent to which innovations should be seen as professional development and learning, which may have a relatively informal structure, or as teacher research that may need to meet certain design criteria, including the establishment of baseline levels. Here there is a trade-off between seeking to incorporate the innovation into regular classroom practice as quickly as possible and more detailed and systematic information at the outset. The professional learning model may operate without any detailed record-keeping, so that any subsequent claims will be based on impressionistic judgements. The research model will involve more preparatory work and data collection that allows stronger claims to be made. This latter approach is essentially an action research design in which a baseline is established, a change ('an intervention') is made and the effects monitored, with adjustments to the approach when necessary. Comparison with the baseline then allows the impact of the change to be described.

### Why innovate?

Many of the projects reviewed in the ARIA study appeared to work from a relatively loose 'need to improve' base. For example, there was tacit recognition for the need to develop more consistency in teachers' summative assessment, for example Qualifications and Curriculum Agency's (QCA's) *Monitoring Pupil Progress* (QCA, 2006b). Those more concerned with formative assessment made the appeal to create successful lifelong learners in an age of rapid change; for example, the DCELLS (2009a) *Thinking and Assessment for Learning Development Programme* and the *Jersey Actioning Formative Assessment* (JAFA) project (Crossouard and Sebba, 2006).

What follows are more detailed examples of approaches to establishing baselines that were used in initiatives examined by the ARIA study. Although these emerged more commonly in large-scale projects, they offer approaches that may, in a scaled-down form, be feasible for teacher researchers who are investigating their own or their colleagues' innovations.

### Using questionnaire data – before and after

The relatively large-scale and longitudinal *Learning How to Learn* study (James et al., 2006a) provides an example of how survey data can be used to monitor impact in a project that sought to initiate and monitor assessment for learning strategies across a network of schools. This has been selected in part because the questionnaires are available (LHTL, 2009) and because it illustrates how questionnaires can be used to monitor impact. The findings are not discussed in any detail and, indeed, if they demonstrate anything, it is that change is rarely clear-cut or smooth.

In order to see if the project had led to any changes in attitude, both among teachers and pupils, three questionnaires were developed (primary pupils, secondary pupils and teachers). These were administered twice, a year apart, to the same individuals. This allowed the researchers to detect changes in attitudes over that period of time and to relate them to what teachers were saying and what the researchers were observing in the classroom. For example, the primary pupil questionnaires had 25 items and used alternative statements (a 'semantic differential approach') about which pupils indicated their opinions on a six-point scale. They were asked to give an opinion on the statements such as:

| | | |
|---|---|---|
| If you produce lots of pages of work it means your work is good | ---------------------- | Just because you've produced a lot of pages of work doesn't mean your work is good' |

Other items included: 'I like to be told exactly what to do —— I like doing things where I can use my own ideas' or 'I don't check my work unless I have to —— I often check my work so I can improve it'. Nine of the items were grouped into a 'school learning' factor with another five items constituting the 'involvement and initiative in learning' factor. The secondary pupils' questionnaire had an additional 20 questions.

The responses of the 200 primary pupils who took the survey twice showed increases in the 'school learning' factor in all the six schools over the year. However the 'involvement and initiative in learning' factor showed only slight increases in half of the schools and slight decreases in the other half. For the 600 Year 8 secondary pupils, changes were twice as large for the 'school learning' factor than for the 'involvement and initiative in learning' factor, but there were gains and losses on both findings. Being increasingly positive about the involvement factor generally led to increased positive findings about school learning. The survey also showed that there were substantial differences between schools in their pupils' responses to the survey.

This represents one way of assessing changes during an initiative. For smaller-scale initiatives 'before and after' interviews or focus groups may be more appropriate approaches. However, the basic aim is the same: finding a means to collect systematic evidence of whether the innovation has led to changes in attitudes and perceptions.

### Pre-innovation attainment levels and control groups

The action research of Black and Wiliam (2003) has already been referred to in earlier chapters but Wiliam et al. (2004) also reported an attempt to establish if there had been an impact on student achievement. An idealized way of doing this would be to conduct pre-tests with both the innovation group and a control group who were matched in key ways, yet not part of the innovation. We do not, however, live in this idealized world. In one local authority initiative, for example, the design included pre- and post-test measures in the schools involved. These took the form of age-standardized tests of reading and mathematics that were given to both the participating classes and to control groups. The impact of this experimental design was weakened by teacher reluctance to use the tests. This was largely because they were in a different format to national curriculum tests and were therefore perceived as of limited value to pupils and teachers as they prepared for the national tests. There was 'nothing in it for us'. Teachers may therefore resist pre- and post-testing if they believe it will add to the test burdens on pupils without bringing any benefit. This was particularly the case with control groups for whom the 'what's in it for us?' question rightly looms large. However, one common methodological device for surmounting this problem is to use a research design in which the experimental and control groups change roles in a second phase of the project.

Knowing these pressures, Wiliam et al. opted for a more naturalistic design, using data that were already in existence or were part of regular summative testing in the classroom:

> We sought to make use of whatever assessment instruments would have been administered by the school in the normal course of events. In many cases, these were the results on the national tests for 14 year olds or the grades on the national school leaving examination (the GCSE), but in some cases we made use of scores from school assessments (particularly in science, where modular approaches meant that scores on end-of-module tests were available).
>
> (Wiliam et al., 2004)

They recognized that this approach has limitations; for example, the tests might lack curricular validity if they did not accurately reflect what had been taught during the innovation. However, the strength of this method was that these assessments were part of normal classroom practice and so there was not the sense of imposition and additional burden that was found in the local authority initiative.

Simply knowing the results of various assessments does not allow much to be said about the impact of the innovation, since they could have been the result of factors other than the formative assessment classroom practices the researchers were studying. This is where control groups become important: are there groups similar the innovation group in everything except the innovative practices that were being studied? If there are, do their results differ?

Wiliam et al. also again looked for a naturalistic solution to setting up control groups:

> In order to be able to interpret the outcomes we discussed the local circumstances in the school with each teacher and set up the best possible comparison group consistent with not disrupting the work of the school. In some cases, we used a parallel class taught by the same or a different teacher or, failing that, a non-parallel class taught by the same or different teacher. We also made use of national norms where these were available.
>
> (Wiliam et al., 2004: 57)

Again there are trade-offs at work here. No two teachers have the same impact and no two classes are the same and so there may be other effects at work that could explain differences in the results. There may also be an issue of the same teacher teaching one class as the experimental group and one as the control, giving rise to 'uncontrolled dissemination'. What helps in the formative assessment class may well then be used by the same teacher in the control class, because it has had a positive impact.

While the statistical analysis in the project was more sophisticated than might be expected of small-scale teacher research (establishing standardized effect sizes, a method that is not without theoretical concerns), it would be possible to develop simpler and more descriptive statistical analyses for classroom research in one or more schools. However, even complex statistical techniques cannot remove some of the imprecision of this naturalistic approach. While the researchers suggested that the use of a parallel or previous class taught by the same teacher was the most robust comparison, this makes assumptions about the classes being similar. For example, this would be problematic if pupils are put in teaching groups based on attainment and teachers take different groups each year; a high-achieving group one year; a lower-achieving group the next. The comparison of different teachers teaching similar classes runs the obvious problem that one teacher may be better than another, with the results reflecting this rather than the impact of the innovation.

The actual findings of the King's, Medway, Oxfordshire Formative Assessment Project (KMOFAP) project illustrated some of this complexity, and again illustrated that impact is rarely straightforward. While overall there was evidence of better performance by the classes exposed to innovative formative assessment innovation, these effects varied from teacher to teacher. There was a statistically significant improvement in performance, relative to the comparison groups, for nine of the 25 teachers with one having a significant decrease in performance. Twelve teachers experienced positive effects for the formative groups that were short of statistical significance, while three had negative effects.

Using these approaches Wiliam et al. were able to claim that the results provided:

> firm evidence that improving formative assessment does produce tangible results in terms of externally mandated assessments. At the very least, these data suggest that teachers do not, as is sometimes reported, have to choose between teaching well and getting good results.
>
> (Wiliam et al., 2004: 63–4)

Considerable emphasis has been placed on *baseline descriptors* and on detailed examples of pre- and post-innovation measures because they were relatively neglected in much of the work we reviewed. While their absence may not be seen as a problem in local settings, in which teachers may have experienced some changes and successes, the lack of systematic data collection means that only the most cautious generalizations are possible. Even these may be subject to alternative explanations, such as the Hawthorne effect, but providing comparative data should help to identify the most plausible explanations.

## 2 Statements of intended outcomes

This is the equivalent of making clear 'where they need to go to' in AfL. What will success look like and how would we recognize it? Innovations are intended to make a difference and the assumption is that those involved will be aware of what they are attempting to do. For example, one large-scale project listed its main aims as

- improving pupil performance;
- increasing engagement with learning;
- changing classroom practice thereby improving pedagogy;
- increasing the frequency of creative lessons.

The first three aims are similar to those found in other AfL initiatives; for example, Scotland's *Assessment is For Learning* (Hayward et al., 2005).

A key issue here is the generality of such intentions and what indicators would show whether they are being met. This relates to the *purpose(s)* of the innovation and how explicit these have been made. The task, therefore, is to declare in advance what kind of outcomes we can expect to see if the innovation is effective. While the examples above are arguably too general to be helpful, they could be made more explicit by providing indicators. For example, in what areas might we see improved pupil performance and how might this be recognized? Similarly, what would constitute specific indicators of increased engagement?

## 3 Evidence of outcomes

The more generalized the statements of intention, the more difficult it may be to provide evidence that the aims of an innovation have been met. This was acknowledged in several of the projects in which some of the aims were judged to have been met. For example, changes in teachers' practices and increased pupil engagement were recorded, whereas others, including improved pupil outcomes, were unable to be evaluated.

Some initiatives present instructive examples of more systematic collection of evidence. Examples included the monitoring of agreement levels in the QCA and Essex local education authority's assessment consistency trials. In the case study of Edisford Primary School, which had won a 'best innovative practice award', there was empirical evidence of impact in the form of improved Key Stage 2 Sat scores, pupil surveys (engagement and enjoyment) and OFSTED comments.

This level of triangulation may be easier for a single school than for a more diffuse project that involves individuals from different schools. However, it raises the question of what the 'success criteria' would look like. For several of the bigger projects, such as the Jersey JAFA project and the Portsmouth AfL project, independent evaluations were commissioned. These allowed some triangulation between teacher perceptions, pupil responses and external documentation. However, for some of the projects the evaluations only began once the project was well established, making it difficult to establish a baseline and appraise the impact of the innovation.

## 4 Unintended consequences

This takes the impact of a project a step further and asks whether the consequences were those that were intended. A published example of this was Smith and Gorard's (2005) report of a school's experiment with comment-only marking (mentioned previously in Chapter 1). The design involved a single experimental class, with the three other mixed ability classes in the year acting as control groups. The experiment was to run for a year and then pre- and post-test scores were compared. Unfortunately, both the teachers and pupils involved had only a limited understanding of the experiment and so it distorted the meaning of comment-only marking. For example, the written feedback was no different from the typical 'good work' comment that often accompanies marks, with one pupil commenting 'Miss, I'd like to know my marks because comments don't tell us much' (p. 33). The pupils similarly were unclear: 'They don't give us our marks. It's supposed to be some sort of project because... we don't have our marks... to see how we react and that' (p. 31). This lack of understanding of, and commitment to, the experiment led to decreased performance, with the control classes doing better in the final tests. The pupils felt disadvantaged by not having marks, with one teacher commenting: 'They were gagging for their marks' (p. 33).

The design and conduct of this experiment attracted considerable criticism from other researchers (e.g., Black et al., 2005a, 2005b) both because of the inadequate training the teachers had received and for its lack of ethical integrity in not stopping it when it was obviously having a detrimental effect. However, almost a year later the underlying flaws in the research design became more apparent when the assistant head of the school reported (Burns, 2006) that Key Stage 3 results for English, mathematics and science had steadily improved, after a systematically more thorough programme of introducing AfL, including support for written feedback.

There is no direct evidence of such unintended consequences in the projects reviewed in the ARIA study. However, several did report negative responses from 'control group' schools, those schools that were outside the project and were used for comparison. The concept of 'unintended consequences' does not necessarily mean that the consequences are unforeseen. We know, for example, that high stakes accountability testing will constrain teaching and learning – so this will be no surprise; it is simply not what the policy had intended.

## 5 Interpretations including alternative explanations

The interpretation of why a project had an observed impact needs to consider if other plausible explanations exist. These could range from such general features as the teachers being more enthusiastic because they were part of a project, receiving attention and resources, to a specific element of the innovation creating the impact while other elements were ineffective.

One feature of the context in which most of the studied projects were taking place was that there were *multiple initiatives* in operation. The Jersey project involved both AfL and critical thinking, and in Wales AfL and thinking skills were brought together. In most schools central initiatives; for example, the primary strategy in England (DCSF, 2009d) would be running alongside other initiatives, both local and national. Under these circumstances how do we apportion the contribution to any improvements within the school or classroom? Any interpretation of the impact of an innovation has to be both cautious and tentative.

## Conclusion

The participants in the innovations reviewed in the ARIA study all believed, to varying degrees, that what they had achieved had made a difference. While the various approaches were all able to show how something 'had worked' for the teachers, there was sometimes a lack of systematic information to triangulate with these perceptions. This raises the question about whether activities conducted as part of professional learning need to take note and promote the kind of data that might be expected for more research-oriented action research.

This chapter has offered some ways in which classroom innovations could provide information that would strengthen claims and allow more generalization beyond the immediate context of the activity. Key steps include the use of baseline information, making the aims of the innovation more explicit and identifying how success would be demonstrated. There is also the need to consider alternative explanations of what had gone on and to be alert for unintended consequences.

Collecting data is time-consuming and can be intrusive. What we have encouraged in this chapter is to look for naturalistic approaches that make use of what is already there, or to use survey methods that make the demands placed on participants as limited as possible. Such approaches will allow for findings to be triangulated, which in turn will allow increasing confidence in the claims being made.

### Questions for reflection

1. To what extent should classroom innovations be expected to meet research design demands?

2. What evidence or indicators are available to describe the pre-innovation practices and standards?

3. How best can the intentions of an innovation be specified in advance of a project to assess its impact?

4. What would constitute valid evidence for a project meeting its intentions?

5. What alternative explanations might be offered?

6. What claims can be made for an innovation in a context of multiple initiatives?

## Note

1. The original experiments at the Hawthorne Works outside Chicago in the 1920s involved varying the lighting for a specially isolated group of shop floor workers. The surprising result was that the dimming and brightening of the lighting both increased productivity for a short time before it returned to normal.

# 9    Embedding and sustaining developments in teacher assessment

*Wynne Harlen and Louise Hayward*

This chapter sets out to identify the characteristics of sustainable change in assessment practice and the conditions that promote it. The concept of good practice in assessment has to be seen as dynamic and evolving, because the schools and teachers involved are changing all the time. Good practice in assessment is constantly changing in order to remain consistent with learning processes and outcomes that are valued at that time and in that context. An important message, therefore, is that for assessment practices to remain supportive of learning, there is a need to create a culture in which assessment practice will change according to context. The prevailing wisdom is that change has to be undertaken with people rather than be done to people. There are many ways to realize the vision that all assessment should support learning. Teachers and schools need the opportunity to work out their own paths if developments in teacher assessment are to be sustained.

## Sustainable development

The focus in this chapter is on sustaining the development of changing practices; practices that are likely to support learners and learning. Yet sustainability is a term often used as if it were a steady state; one where current practices are continued over time or where new 'good' practices once implemented and disseminated are fixed for a long period locally, nationally or internationally.

Cullingford (2004), writing on sustainability education, poses an interesting question: Is sustainability sustainable? He argues that there are two interconnected levels to the concept of sustainability, scientific and moral. If we reflect on these ideas in relation to assessment, what Cullingford describes as the scientific aspect might involve sustaining the development of assessment practices, rooted in research evidence and contextualized in the everyday circumstances of working with different learners in different contexts. The moral aspect of sustainability is more complicated. Cullingford's analysis of sustainability in education relates to university education but we would suggest that there are strong parallels with assessment in schools. He argues that 'All are involved in the consequences of other people's actions. Sustainability involves issues that are about competing interests and values, but not from a position of choice. The need to work together is mandatory' (p. 247).

Sustaining new practice in education is inherently a dynamic process. Institutions, organizations and people are changing all the time. Even the concept of good practice is problematic and has to be seen as dynamic and evolving, dependent on time and context. What we can say is that good practice at a particular time and in a particular context is consistent with facilitating certain learning processes and outcomes that are valued at that time and in that context. Variation is therefore expected in what is desirable practice from one situation to another and over time.

In education, and specifically in assessment, the notion of sustaining unchanging practice is inappropriate. Classroom procedures and activities, which may seem new and useful at one time, soon become a drab routine and no longer meet the ever-changing needs of teachers and students. The reasons for what is done become lost. In formative assessment, for example, ideas from research have been developed into a range of strategies to be used in schools and classrooms. The link between ideas and practice is central but often appears difficult to sustain. Some teachers will implement new practices with understanding the underlying ideas, while others will inevitably use new approaches that work, with less understanding of why they work. Consequently, some teachers may describe what they do as assessment for learning (AfL) or formative assessment just because they are using certain techniques. Their formative assessment becomes a series of procedures; for example, they use 'two stars and a wish', 'traffic lights' and 'wait time'. Unless adapted and used flexibly as strategies to promote greater understanding of learning among learners, then these practices soon become ossified and reduced in effectiveness. This tendency towards reducing complex processes to relatively simple elements (reductionism) leads to a fracture between practice and underlying principles, between research and classrooms.

Instead, we have to think of change as ongoing, as finding different ways of ensuring that new needs and new goals are met. Looked at in this light, sustainability will require those who are close to the action to make informed decisions about what action is appropriate. Another way of putting this is that the process of change is embedded in practice.

However, embedding change in practice is a complicated business. Creating the conditions for those who are close to action to take informed decisions will involve teachers, researchers and policy makers working together.

It is important not to separate people from ideas. Nothing will be developed without people; for example, teachers, researchers, policy makers, pupils, politicians and parents. The climate in which any development takes place is likely to be a crucial factor in whether or not development is sustained. If members of any group, for example teachers, feel themselves to be outsiders, overloaded or disempowered, their ability to enact and to sustain development is likely to be compromised. How people feel about their own learning, their role in their own learning, their ability to influence what happens in the development, how it relates to what they believe and what they already do are all important factors to consider from the beginning of a development that aspires to be sustainable.

## What is to be sustained?

The previous section might be taken to suggest that what we want to sustain is a process of constant development in response to change in students' needs and learning contexts. Of course it has to be more than that. The direction of change and the reasons for change, based on underlying values, are the substance of what to change. The overarching aim in assessment reform is to use assessment to ensure that students have optimum opportunities to learn. Earlier chapters in this book have suggested how developments in assessment can contribute to increasingly effective learning environments. These involve, for example:

- reflective practitioners who are consistently engaged in their own professional learning;
- commitment of those involved, whether directly as teachers or more indirectly as administrators, advisers or parents, to effective pedagogical practices and their understanding of what makes them effective, in comparison with alternative practices;
- teachers supporting each other in continuing to develop ways of using assessment and other aspects of teaching purposefully and flexibly;
- sufficient flexibility in the vision of what is required for those involved to adapt it to their context while retaining key features;
- commitment to the active role of learners in their own learning.

These characteristics of effective learning environments are, in effect, characteristics of sustainable development; flexible, adaptable professionalism at individual and collaborative levels of engagement. We can look to examples of assessment reform, past and present, to see how these and other features of sustained change can be put into practice.

Senge et al. (2005) argue that change is both an individual and a collective process. Thus, change that is sustainable beyond individual learners or individual teachers must involve change within communities, such as schools, and across communities, through policy. What can be done to change the practice of individual teachers, or even schools, is not enough to maintain change in a whole system. For this, changes may well be needed in teacher education programmes, in policies, in criteria used in school evaluation by schools themselves and by inspectors, in funding arrangements, and so on.

## Conditions associated with sustained change: evidence from past projects and present practice

Identifying conditions that have favoured or inhibited sustainable development requires us to examine cases where change in assessment has been sustained and where it has not. Past examples are useful since retrospection shows us to what extent the change was or was not sustained and allows us to begin to analyse the reasons why. Looking back also suggests that it is important to distinguish between changes in practice that comply with 'the letter' and those that reflect 'the spirit' of what is required. In addition, previous developments enable us to consider practices that have been sustained with little effort long past their 'sell by' date and which form an obstacle to change.

### National curriculum assessment

It is undeniable that national curriculum assessment in England, introduced in 1991, constitutes a change that has been sustained in one form or another. This is largely, of course, because it is statutory. The Task Group on Assessment and Testing (TGAT) (DES/WO, 1988) intended that there should be national testing and teachers' assessment at the end of key stages. These were originally intended to serve both formative and summative assessment purposes. In looking only at what has been sustained, we therefore need to consider these two purposes separately.

In relation to summative assessment, the teacher assessment element depended on teachers' judgements and had the potential to enhance teachers' professionalism. Hall and Harding (2002) researched how Key Stage 1 teachers conducted their summative assessment and reported observing two main approaches, which they described as 'collaborative' and 'individualistic'. Collaborative schools showed acceptance of the goals of the assessment; they shared among staff their interpretation of the criteria (level descriptions), planned the collection of data and adopted a common language in discussing assessment. Teachers in these schools perceived their assessment to be having a positive impact on teaching and learning. By contrast, individualistic schools were reluctant to comply, and in some cases resistant; there was little sharing of views, people were confused about terms and assessment was 'bolted on'. Not surprisingly, teachers in these schools saw assessment as imposed and of little value in the classroom. The key difference between these groups was the willingness of the 'collaborators' to accept the goals and work together with others to find ways of putting them into practice in their particular situations. At first this appeared to be a key factor leading to the intended positive impact on the learning environment.

However, practice in the 'collaborative' schools became less so as time went on. There was generally no allowance of time for collaboration and moderation of teacher assessment to take place and other pressures, particularly after the 1997 introduction of the national literacy and numeracy strategies, began to absorb teachers' attention. According to Hall and Harding (2002: 13), 'The fact that funding was not made available for teachers to moderate the TA results served to tell teachers that the results of the external testing programme were prioritized over TA'. Using teacher assessment could have enhanced teachers' professionalism but its diminished status threatened that sense of professionalism.

Even in those schools initially willing to make changes that enabled assessment to be used to help learning, the lack of continued support for this meant that the practice died out. Thus, formative assessment was not sustained in national curriculum assessment. Teachers' summative assessment continued, since it was required, but it did not serve the intended purpose because implementing it was given far less attention than was given to preparing students for the national tests. The production of non-statutory tests for non-core subjects and for year groups other than the end of key stages further militated against the development of good summative assessment by teachers.

What we might learn from this is that if we are concerned with sustaining a change in 'spirit' and not just in 'the letter', some conditions are needed to support the initial response of the 'collaborative' schools. These include time for teachers to work out with others how to incorporate the assessment into their work and time for the process to be conducted so that summative judgements are dependable. Most importantly, the product has to be valued for the particular contribution it can make to reporting on student learning. It is a matter of conjecture that, supposing the conditions for collaboration had been maintained, the practices in the collaborative schools would have 'infected' the individualistic schools through contacts between and movements of staff. It is clear, however, that if lack of discussion time has a negative influence even in 'collaborative' cultures, 'individualistic' ones are likely to need even more opportunities to think, meet and discuss new developments. Time to think matters through is needed as a continuing part of the process and not simply at the beginning. Indeed, time to reflect would seem to be a key characteristic of any development in which integrity is sustained. The importance of policy coherence is also highlighted by the Assessment Reform Group (ARG, 2006) and Harlen (2007). Even within the same policy framework, different parts interact and can have a negative impact on one another.

## The Foundation Stage Profile

The Early Years Foundation Stage Profile (EYFSP), introduced in England in 2003, is another statutory assessment intended to serve both formative and summative purposes (QCA, 2008b). Since it applies to children aged 3–5, it depends on observations of children during regular activities over time. Observations are made in relation to all areas of learning identified in the early learning goals. Summative judgements are made at the end of the Foundation Stage using nine points within 13 scales relating to the goals. The EYFSP is based on the assumption that early years practitioners will build up evidence for their assessments from ongoing teaching and learning throughout the reception year, and that they will be able to make most judgements for each scale on the basis of this accumulated evidence. If the profile is not built in this way, the potential for formative use is lost and completing the record for every child is inevitably seen as a heavy burden. Moderation within a Foundation Stage setting is intended to enable all those in contact with a child to contribute to the summative judgement. Moderation across settings is also necessary so that common standards are used in the records that are passed to Year 1 teachers.

For the formative value of the EYFSP to be realized, there has to be time for practitioners to become familiar with the scales and to experience the benefit of collecting and using evidence as an ongoing process. Otherwise, the EYFSP could be seen as a time-consuming requirement of little value. This perception is often underlined by the reaction of Year 1 teachers to the information provided. If Year 1 teachers are unfamiliar with the Foundation Stage goals and how the detailed profiles have been built up, they may not value the information they receive. This indicates a need to consider other parts of the system when changes are being made in one part.

The value of a new assessment such as the EYFSP has to be recognized by teachers through experience; it is not enough simply to claim that it is of benefit. The EYFSP was presented to most teachers as a completed instrument, so it was not easy for them to feel ownership. It takes time for teachers to fit the new requirements into their work and their existing assessment practice, a process helped by teachers understanding the principles behind a change and having some flexibility in applying these principles to their own circumstances.

As with the example from national curriculum assessment in England, it is clear that for a development to be sustainable the link between purpose and practice has to be maintained. It is also clear that opportunities for teachers to think ideas through into practice and to develop ideas using feedback from practice are important.

### Graded assessment schemes

Graded assessment schemes were an earlier assessment innovation in England and Wales, developed in the late 1980s in several subjects including mathematics, modern foreign languages and science. The schemes organized assessment in the secondary school into a sequence of tests at progressively more advanced levels. In science there were 15 levels of achievement and students started at level 1 in the first year and worked through the levels until their fifth year. The final level reached was intended to determine the GCSE grade. The upper seven levels of the scheme had equivalents in GCSE grades and the whole course could, with approval from the then Schools Examination and Assessment Council, replace the two-year GCSE course. A pupil record sheet provided students with information about their performance in skills, content and explorations. The schemes held advantages for many students as they removed the single examination in the fifth year of secondary school (Year 11) and maintained motivation for most students throughout the five years. However, the frequency of tests was high – about once every four weeks – and for the less highly achieving students the system could produce a feeling of helplessness as they fell progressively further behind their peers.

The schemes had the potential to meet some of the requirements for formative assessment and incorporate the advantages of progressive assessment. But while still under development, they were brought to an end by the introduction of the national curriculum and national assessment. There are two lessons to be learned here. The first is that assessment systems have to be designed to support all learners. There can be little educational integrity in a system that advantages one group of learners and disadvantages others. The second is that, to be sustained, new assessment practices have to be consistent with national assessment policy and may not remain so if that changes.

# What can we learn from innovations since 2000?

As part of the ARIA study that underlies this book, educationalists from across the UK, who had been involved in innovations in assessment, came together to discuss their experiences. Those involved in helping teachers change their practice suggested that teachers were more likely to adopt and to continue practice if it helped them with problems that they had. This is a factor identified by Senge and Scharmer (2001) as significant in research on transformational change. For action to be taken the problem has to be recognized as important and the effort to solve it must be con- sidered worth while. For instance, teachers may not recognize that they need to improve their summative assessment as long as tests are treated as the most important means of providing summative information. On the other hand, years of experience of tests and their impact on students and teaching may bring realization that their own summative assessment is a better alternative. Their 'problem' then becomes related to how to do it; that is, how to collect and turn evidence into judgements.

In relation to adopting and sustaining formative assessment, there may be a different reason; for example, to engage students in learning, to get them to take some responsibility for their assessment and decisions about improving their work. In this context, teachers need to know how to turn evidence from students' learning into action to help that learning. The promise that formative assessment can help with these problems can be the motivation for individual teachers to adopt relevant new practices. And it is only through change made by individual teachers that new prac- tice can be sustained across a group, school or system.

Thus, the motivation for change in summative assessment and forma- tive assessment may arise in different ways and for this reason we consider them separately.

## Change in summative assessment

In the King's Oxfordshire Summative Assessment Project (KOSAP) (Black et al., 2006a) teachers were motivated to improve summative assessment by the negative impacts of current procedures on students and teachers. Initially, the project worked with secondary subject teachers who were familiar with formative assessment. Rather than starting from intended outcomes, they began their consideration of summative assessment by addressing the question of 'what it means to be good' in, say, mathematics or English. Then attention was given to collecting adequate and convincing evidence of how good students are. It appeared that the sources of evidence that teachers preferred varied with the subject, although the project hoped to extend the range of evidence used by all. The concern for reliability led some teachers to want to introduce 'controlled' pieces of work, designed to provide a focus for assessment of particular outcomes by individual students. The prevalence of group work made it difficult to rely entirely on evidence from regular class work. The project did not collect evidence of the reliability of the outcomes of teacher assessment.

The development of controlled or special tasks was one focus of the Key Stage 3 Assessing Pupils' Progress (APP) project in English (QCA, 2006b) and mathematics. The APP project has produced a bank of tasks for teachers to use as and when they seem appropriate, in order to supplement teachers' understanding of what their pupils have achieved. In addition, there is guidance to help teachers to make judgements of a collection of students' ongoing work at any time during Key Stage 3. The guidance material, developed through pilot trials, identifies the characteristics of work meeting the 'assessment focuses' for national curriculum descriptions of attainment at a particular level and provides exemplars of assessed work. Record sheets were also provided for teachers to make cumulative records of their judgements about each assessment focus and so arrive at the overall level for each student at the end of the key stage. The record shows where individual students need further help and at the same time reveals to teachers areas of work that may have received insufficient attention in their programme of work. In these respects, the materials could be said to provide formative feedback to teachers.

The role of APP materials has been significantly changed by the decision to end national testing at the end of Key Stage 3 from 2009. With teacher assessment as the only basis for reporting achievement, the APP has an important function in improving reliability. If Key Stage 3 tests were still in operation, the APP might well be seen as burdensome, whereas with teacher assessment moving to the front line they are seen as helping to solve 'the problem' of confidence in the results. Again, as in the case of graded assessment, policy decisions clearly impact on how new procedures are viewed and whether they continue to be used.

The aim to introduce APP materials into the primary school is also likely to be influenced by the context in which they are introduced. Changes to improve teachers' summative assessment through the APP materials, and the introduction of special tasks to ensure that the programme of learning includes a wide range of opportunities, will depend on decisions about national tests. With the recent publication of the Rose curriculum review (Rose, 2009) and the report of the Expert Group on Assessment (DCSF, 2009c), it will be interesting to see how the concerns of teachers play out against the government's determination to use measures of pupil outcomes for evaluating schools. The importance given to tests as a basis for target-setting and the continued existence of high stakes tests at the end of Key Stage 2 for English and mathematics could overshadow teachers' summative assessment for these subjects. However, for science at Key Stage 2, the discontinuation of tests in 2010 and their replacement by teacher assessment, based on the use of APP materials, and some special tasks, may well raise the profile of APP (see Chapter 3). On the other hand, if concerns that the end of testing is a symptom of downgrading of science are borne out, then less attention may be paid to the results.

The political context is also relevant to understanding how change may be sustained. In Wales, for example, the change from external testing to full dependence on teacher assessment could be made with relative ease. National testing was discontinued for 7-year-olds in 2002, for 11-year-olds in 2005 and for 14-year-olds in 2006. Since the ending of statutory tests 'optional assessment materials' have been circulated to all schools as an aid to consistency in 'levelling' the performance of students at ages 7 and 11. Not surprisingly, perhaps, since teachers were used to depending on tests, Collins et al. (2008) have reported evidence of continued use of test data for reporting, for cohort target-setting within schools and as a basis for negotiation of targets between schools and local authorities. However, moderation procedures are being implemented to focus more on improving teacher assessment than on using tests. Two different models of moderation are being established.

The first model, at Key Stage 2, is of cluster group moderation whereby each comprehensive school is linked to a number of associated primary schools. Teachers meet on designated in service training (INSET) days, to work on standardizing their judgements for Year 6 students with a view to facilitating transfer. The second, at Key Stage 3, is based on school accreditation in which schools submit sample portfolios of pupil work in every national curriculum subject for scrutiny and feedback at the national level. When schools have demonstrated that they have the procedures in place to ensure consistency of judgement, they become accredited to conduct assessment without external moderation.

Daugherty (2009) explains how the changes have been adopted in terms of the social and political context in Wales:

> They are only possible in a social and political context where the vision statement for the education system includes:
>
> 'The informed professional judgement of teachers, lecturers and trainers must be celebrated without prejudice to the disciplines of

public accountability; and with proper regard to clearing the way to unleash the capacity and expertise of practitioners'.

(NAfW, 2001: 11)

Daugherty also quotes Drakeford's (2007) argument that one of the defining principles in Wales is that 'in the design, delivery and improvement of public services, co-operation is better than competition' (p. 6).

## Change in relation to formative assessment

While improvement in teachers' summative assessment requires change in something that teachers already do, in the case of formative assessment the position is often to introduce practices that are seen as new or at least substantially different from existing ones. For instance, while the way in which teachers give feedback to their students may need to be changed, they may do little in relation to communicating goals of learning or arranging for students' self- and peer-assessment.

In the Assessment for Learning project in Northern Ireland, introduced in 2004, the practices were clearly new to many teachers. The Council for Curriculum, Examinations and Assessment (CCEA, 2006) carried out an evaluation by using a questionnaire sent to the teachers and principals in the 55 primary and secondary schools then involved. The survey found that over one-third of the 69 respondents felt that the approaches were not suitable for all pupils and over a half of those involved showed 'some resistance', presumably a way of saying that the approaches were rejected. Although many were enthusiastic about the response of students (e.g. more confident, persevering, aware of what they had to do) and the effect on teaching (e.g. more focused on students' needs), there were many who were unconvinced of the advantages. The evaluation indicated that communication about the project, both to the schools and within the schools, was a likely cause of concern. Many teachers were not aware of the potential benefits of and reasons for using formative assessment and schools did not provide the time for them to plan to implement the project effectively. Relevant school policies needed to be changed and parents needed to be informed of the changes taking place. It appeared that the conditions for sustaining change within a school were not in place at this early stage and lessons had to be learned if wider implementation was to produce sustainable change. Attention clearly needed to be given to teachers' pleas for more time for planning, sharing and reflection.

In Wales the Developing Thinking and Assessment for Learning Programme was set up in 2005 to bring together two strategies that had been shown separately to improve performance and motivation for learning. The programme ended in 2008 and some indications as to whether it is likely to be sustained can be gained from the evaluation carried out towards the end of the programme by Kellard et al. (2008) at the request of DCELLS. The data, collected by a series of questionnaires during the development of the programme, school visits and discussion with the nine local authority advisers involved in the development, presented a highly positive response to the programme. It was found that there was an increase in the number of children participating in discussion, in their confidence and in their enjoyment of learning. During the short period covered by the evaluation, no definite evidence of improved attainment was found but classroom practice was reported as giving more emphasis to effective questioning, encouraging learners to reflect on how they learned and an increase in formative feedback accompanied by a decrease in giving marks or grades.

From Kellard et al.'s evaluation, the following can be inferred about the conditions likely to favour sustaining the programme after the end of the development:

- the importance of the enthusiasm, support and active involvement of senior management;
- help for teachers to try some practical strategies from which their theoretical understanding could follow;
- flexibility in the programme so that schools can develop their own approaches without feeling that they were making mistakes;
- additional funding to allow both those teachers new to the programme and the more experienced to reflect on and evaluate their implementation of the strategies;
- the opportunity for teachers to talk about their practice to others from different schools.

The evaluation noted that the 'hands-off' approach of DCELLS was a positive feature in enabling schools to take the lead and ownership of the programme – a lesson that other more interfering administrations could well heed.

In Scotland, assessment reform began when a review of assessment was published by HMI in 1999. The review suggested that there had been little progress in putting into practice the Assessment 5–14 guidelines published in 1991. The Minister for Education in Scotland commissioned a consultation to seek views on the future of assessment in Scotland. The review concluded that the assessment policy that placed a strong emphasis on the importance of teachers' professional judgement should be sustained. The problems lay in putting the policy into practice. The Assessment is for Learning (AifL) programme was initiated to try to improve this situation by bringing together understandings from research, policy and practice in assessment. The programme design was influenced by assessment research, particularly that of Black and Wiliam (1998a) and Black et al. (2003); research on what matters for change to be successful, for example, Fullan (2003) and Senge and Scharmer (2001); and the outcome of the consultation. Thus, certain values about how to create and sustain change were built in from the start. The AifL programme was concerned to develop a national assessment system for the age range 3–14. This included assessment for formative and summative purposes, self-evaluation of schools and national monitoring of standards, with an overall intention for feedback at all levels to be used continuously to inform improvements.

In their study of the formative assessment component of AifL, Hayward and Spencer (2006) reported three conditions that appeared to promote successful change in teachers' formative assessment practice. First, ideas had to be perceived to have educational integrity, to focus on improving pupils' learning. Second, for changes to become deeply embedded, they had to have personal and professional integrity: teachers had to feel that the ideas were consistent with their own educational value positions and that they were being developed in ways that recognized the teacher as professional, not as an implementer of other people's ideas. Third, ideas had to be consistent both within and across communities; teachers had to feel supported by the system rather than in conflict with it. At the school level, policy had to be consistent with the innovation and, beyond school, it was important that quality assurance systems sought evidence that was consistent with what the innovation required of the teachers and school.

There are many threats to sustainability and the relationship between research, practice and policy is complicated. In particular, how policy is translated into practice depends on the relationship between policy makers and practitioners. For example, mistrust by teachers of the policy context can lead to lack of engagement with or subversion of the ideas behind a particular policy. When a new national assessment policy was introduced in Scotland in the 1990s, teachers' professional judgements were clearly identified as of prime importance. But the teachers' perception was that the real policy agenda was school performance; what mattered were test results and thus teachers' professional judgement was not seen as important. In contrast to the teacher-empowering design of the policy, teachers almost perversely continued with testing. This perception was informed not only by the context of other policies in Scotland at that time but also by what was observed to be happening in other parts of the UK.

The perceived consistency of policies in assessment is an important factor in sustaining change and development. In Scotland, all the curriculum and assessment guidance is non-statutory but is closely followed. It is important, therefore, that these widely used documents are consistent in the values they espouse and in the ways in which they are put into practice. Accountability systems such as school inspection visits and reports will have an impact on practice. For example, if school inspectors ask only for test data, then the test data would be perceived to be what mattered and teachers' professional judgements would be seen as less important. What happens in one school during an inspection is swiftly and effectively communicated across schools. If there are perceived to be gaps between inspectors' expectations and assessment policy, many schools will seek to respond to what was identified as the real policy agenda. The position is further complicated by miscommunication between inspectors and schools. For example, take the case of a school inspector who observes a school engaging in formative assessment strategies but judges that the teachers are unable to relate the strategies to a broader understanding of learning and assessment or that they do not appear to understand why they are using the strategies. The inspector might then make a critical remark about the school's assessment activities. This criticism may then be misperceived as school inspectors being antagonistic to the new assessment policy. Trust across communities is crucial to sustainability; the lower the trust base the greater the risk of misunderstanding and the greater the threat to sustainability.

Further risks to sustainability lie in the plethora of innovations that have dogged national education systems. The belief that education can influence society in positive ways is a welcome value position; its nemesis is that education has been overburdened with initiative after initiative-seeking to solve the ills of society. Future sustainability of important ideas in assessment may depend on a strategic shift in thinking at policy level. There need to be clear, consistent priorities for curriculum, assessment and pedagogy. Evidence is emerging that this is beginning to happen (see Chapter 3). There needs to be a deeper understanding of what matters to ensure the engagement of all concerned in order to support learners and learning more effectively. Deep and radical change in assessment breaks the boundaries of curriculum and pedagogy. Learning that is sustainable is likely to involve developments across all three and involve personal and professional learning, collective learning in schools, in local communities and authorities, in and across nations.

## What can we learn from practice?

Bringing together factors that seem to support particular practices, the following are among those that apply in some, but not all examples:

- There is consistency between different parts within the whole assessment system.

- The necessary resources are available to sustain and develop the intended practice.
- Teachers and others have evidence of positive impact on student learning.
- The information provided through assessment is useful to and valued by those receiving it.
- There are regular opportunities for teachers, head teachers and others to discuss their assessment practice and to learn from each other.
- The school policy and organization provide the necessary support for teachers to use assessment for and of learning effectively.
- Professional development in assessment is ongoing, in recognition that effective work requires 'continuing drive'.
- Students are aware of their role in assessment.

It is clear that these do not apply in all cases. The one overarching condition seems to be that teachers see what they are doing as worth while and consistent both with the goals of learning that they value and with national goals.

## Is development in assessment sustainable?

This is a difficult question to answer. Cullingford's (2004) analysis of sustainability as having both scientific and moral dimensions may help us to tease out some of the issues. For development in assessment to be sustainable, there is a need to recognize the interaction between the scientific and the moral, between the practices continuously being developed and their moral purpose. Practice, research and policy communities have to acknowledge (and to collaborate to address) the competing interests and values that exist across different communities. This purposeful collaboration would be evident both in the rhetoric and in the actions of researchers, policy makers and practitioners. For example, if at the heart of sustainable development in assessment lies a moral imperative to offer all learners a good educational experience, one designed to equip them to be confident, enabled citizens, then there are clear implications for curriculum, assessment and pedagogy. Teachers, researchers and policy makers would all have roles to play. It would be the teachers' moral responsibility to focus assessment on learners and learning, to work with research communities to create an environment where practical actions are grounded in current knowledge and understandings, and to work with policy communities to promote a culture in which potentially damaging aspects of the use of assessment information for wider purposes of accountability are minimized. It would be a moral responsibility for researchers to work with teachers and with policy makers to develop and to deepen understandings of curriculum, assessment and pedagogy and to work through the possible implications of findings with both groups. Policy makers would have a moral responsibility to work with teachers, researchers and with politicians to develop educationally sound ways of meeting the information demands of education as a public service. Finally, all groups would recognize that, individually and collectively, they have a moral responsibility to build public understanding of education, and in particular of the uses and misuses of assessment information, to campaign for an enhanced public awareness of assessment.

There are parallels here with the process of formative assessment. In formative assessment teachers collect and use evidence to adapt the learning environment to the students' responses and needs. It is a regulatory system with feedback (just as there is feedback in self-regulating systems) ensuring that what is done meets requirements at a particular time and informs future action. If development in assessment is to be sustainable the same process should underpin it. Across the UK there is increasing emphasis on self-regulation as part of the monitoring and evaluation of education systems. In a system where assessment development is sustainable, researchers, policy makers and practitioners would constantly monitor learning and the policies and practices that are intended to support it. They would use the feedback from that process to ensure that assessment is matched to the needs of students, the curriculum and learning that is valued.

We are as yet some way from this. There are seeds of such practice beginning to emerge in some of the projects examined in the ARIA study, projects in which:

- policy makers, researchers and practitioners are trying to cross traditional boundaries and begin to listen to one another, to recognize the competing values and interests that exist within and across the different communities;
- teachers talk of the energizing effect of participative models of development, of feeling liberated from a culture where they were told what to do and how to do it.

We have moved some way from a model that suggested the journey from innovation, supported by professional development, to dissemination and sustainability could be clearly delineated. Nevertheless, many challenges remain to be faced. For example, how can a culture committed to better informed educational policies and practices be sustained; one where feedback is used to inform future learning and where dynamism is constant but does not lead to impossible workloads? Perhaps keeping a clear focus on 'what matters' and not being distracted into self-serving systems, in which data are often collected but not used, might be a useful first step. However, at least we are beginning to ask questions about what sustainable development is, why it matters and what it might look like.

The Sustainable Development Commission's (SD, 2005) five-year strategy on sustainable development is entitled *One Future – Different Paths* and talks of the importance of sustainable communities that embody the principles of sustainable development at the local level. It advocates greater power and say for communities in decisions that affect them and stresses the importance of working in partnership to get things done. This is a more complex model than the one that has dominated recent thinking, in which ideas from a central source would simply be communicated to others, and has the potential to support sustainable development in assessment. It is significant that the Standards for Assessment Practice in Chapter 2 are standards for all communities. It is heartening to think that perhaps we are beginning to learn to live with the complexities of collaboration. There really is no alternative.

## Questions for reflection

1. What are the main factors that need attention within a school, community or local authority if new assessment practices are to be sustained?

2. How may the assessment practices of one teacher, school or local authority have a positive impact on others?

3. When change in assessment practice is a requirement, what needs to be done to ensure that the spirit and rationale of the change is maintained as well as the required procedures?

# Appendix 1

# Projects examined and members of the core group and advisory committee of the Nuffield Foundation-funded Analysis and Review of Innovations in Assessment (ARIA) Study, 2006/8

## A list of the main projects reviewed under the auspices of ARIA

- Assessment is for Learning (Learning and Teaching Scotland and the Scottish Government)
- Assessing Pupils' Progress (Key Stage 3) and Monitoring Children's Progress (Key Stage 2) (Qualifications and Curriculum Authority with the Primary and Secondary National Strategies)
- Assessment for Learning in the Northern Ireland Revised Curriculum (Council for Curriculum, Examinations and Assessment (CCEA), Northern Ireland)
- Consulting Pupils on the Assessment of their Learning (Queen's University, Belfast)
- Programme for Developing Thinking and Assessment for Learning (Department for Children, Education, Lifelong Learning and Skills, Welsh Assembly Government)
- Assessment Programme for Wales: Securing Key Stage 2 and Key Stage 3 Teacher Assessment (Department for Children, Education, Lifelong Learning and Skills, Welsh Assembly Government)
- Project e-Scape. Goldsmiths, University of London
- Jersey Actioning Formative Assessment (JAFA) (King's College London and the Education Department of Jersey)
- King's Medway Oxfordshire Formative Assessment Project (KMOFAP) (King's College, London, Oxfordshire LA and Medway LA)

- King's Oxfordshire Summative Assessment Project (KOSAP) (King's College, London and Oxfordshire LA)
- Learning How to Learn (University of Cambridge)
- Portsmouth Learning Community: Assessment for Learning Strand (Portsmouth LA)
- Summative Teacher Assessments at the End of Key Stage 2 (Birmingham LA and Oxfordshire LA)

*Note*: This list does not include details of the many important local initiatives that featured in ARIA events, for example, promoted by Gateshead Local Authority, Belfast Education and Library Board and the Highland Council (Scotland).

## ARIA Project Core Group and Advisory Committee

*Core Group*

| | |
|---|---|
| John Gardner | Queen's University and Assessment Reform Group, ARG |
| Wynne Harlen | University of Bristol and Assessment Reform Group, ARG |
| Louise Hayward | University of Glasgow and Assessment Reform Group, ARG |
| Gordon Stobart | Institute of Education, London and Assessment Reform Group, ARG |

*Advisory Committee*

| | |
|---|---|
| Paul Black | King's College London and ARG |
| Richard Daugherty | Cardiff University and ARG |
| Kathryn Ecclestone | Oxford Brookes University and ARG |
| Mary James | Institute of Education, London and ARG |
| Dorothy Kavanagh | Assessment Consultant, Oxfordshire |
| Alison Kidd | Quality Improvement Officer, City of Edinburgh |
| Stuart Merry | Emley First School, Huddersfield |
| Martin Montgomery | Formerly Assessment Development Manager, NICCEA |
| Paul Newton | Qualifications and Curriculum Authority and ARG |
| Catrin Roberts | Nuffield Foundation (until 2007) |
| Mike Walker | King Edward VI Grammar School, Chelmsford |
| Anne Whipp | Welsh Assembly Government |

*Project Research Support*

| | |
|---|---|
| Debie Galanouli | Queen's University (January 2007–February 2008) |
| Jo Wilson | Queen's University (September–December 2006) |

# Appendix 2

# A professional development template

*John Gardner*

Most of what we advocate in this book relates to the promotion of innovative change in assessment in schools, through helping the individual teacher to develop his or her own practices. The questions at the end of each chapter are therefore designed to facilitate deeper thinking about the issues raised and the insights offered. They imply the need to get beneath the rhetoric of 'change', 'good practice' and 'reflective practice', to go beyond the mere following of suggestions and guidance to in-depth self-assimilation of the purpose and meaning of the change.

There is a variety of one-to-one models of professional development that can avail of these questions as prompts for discussion. These include mentoring, coaching, modelling and co-teaching. However, the design being proposed here is for a form of collaborative group inquiry with mutually supported action in trying out ideas and new practices. As Chapter 6 sets out, key dimensions of any successful professional development activities will include strong leadership endorsement, appropriate resourcing, engagement by the teachers at all stages and opportunities to experiment.

With these provisos, this appendix offers a simple 'snowball' template for collaborative group inquiry whether in a school or in a cross-school setting such as a local authority continuing professional development (CPD) event. A 'snowball' event is one in which the unit of discussion progressively increases (like a snowball rolling down a snow-covered hillside). This proceeds from individuals to pairs to foursomes to the whole group in a structured series of discussion opportunities.

Depending on the nature and context of the setting, some questions may be more relevant than others. The extent of reading required will also depend to some degree on the setting but mostly it will be the case that the chapter in question will provide the main stimulus for discussion. Clearly, other sources will provide additional, even alternative, insights and these may enrich the process. We recommend careful scrutiny of the References section for materials to extend the participants' knowledge base and breadth of perspective.

A 'snowball' session would typically involve 20 participants and should proceed as follows:

## Pre-reading:

- This will include the chapter that addresses the topic of the session and any appropriate materials or publications from the reference list.
- The pre-reading should be provided at least one week in advance of the session.

## Initial stage:

- The facilitator(s) should enable participants to discuss as a whole group what they hope to achieve from the session. This should be expressed in terms of questions to answers.
- This stage may take 20 minutes or more and it is important not to rush or over-manage it. The session must proceed on the basis of what the participants want.
- The end-of-chapter questions should *not* be allowed to dominate the discussion as it would not be surprising if the participants' aspirations did not coincide completely with them.
- However, the questions do encapsulate the issues raised in the chapters so they should continue to act as a basis on which to work, suitably amended and contextualized to ensure a good fit with the participants' wishes and needs.
- When the content of the key questions has been agreed by the participants, they should be made visible and accessible throughout the subsequent discussions by whatever means is convenient (projection, handouts, etc).

## Snowball stage 1:

- Participants should be facilitated to reflect individually on the questions for 10 minutes.
- During this time they should note anything relevant that they think is important including personal perspectives, 'questions on the questions' (e.g. for clarification), ideas to share, relevant experiences and classroom relevance.

### Snowball stage 2:

- Participants should be facilitated to join in pairs to discuss each other's notes on the questions, in a session period of approximately 20 minutes.
- It is generally a good idea to ensure that there is a good mix within the pairs; for example, by gender, age, subject discipline or pupil phase (e.g. Key Stage 1 or Key Stage 2). However, this is not an imperative.
- Generally, this one-on-one discussion will resolve some 'questions on the questions' while others will be refined for further discussion. The sharing of ideas, experiences, perspectives and views on classroom relevance will find varying degrees of consensus and overlap, while individualistic aspects will remain discrete.
- The joint notes should proceed to the next stage.

### Snowball stage 3:

- The participants should be facilitated to join in groups of four (i.e. joining two pairs) to discuss the pairs' and individuals' contributions.
- This part of the session may take 30 minutes or more to complete.
- A verbal report, with key points on a flipchart or other medium, will be needed from each group of four covering at least the following:
  - relevance of the questions and their focuses to the classroom;
  - interesting ideas and experiences for sharing;
  - proposed practical activities for trying out;
  - proposed follow-up to evaluate the new activities.
- To facilitate the reporting back and recording of key points each group should nominate a key point writer and a rapporteur (the roles could be combined but the spirit of collaborative inquiry would usually demand as much sharing as possible).

At this point there have been at least 80 minutes of intense discussion and there will probably be signs that participants need a little bit of time for reflection and assimilation of the various issues raised, and most importantly a comfort break!

### Snowball stage 4:

- This stage should facilitate whole group (or plenary) discussion of all the various insights, experiences, ideas and remaining questions, as presented by each group of four in turn.

- There is virtue in brevity in this reporting back stage, primarily because of the number of groups (e.g. in this case five groups of four). However, time must be allowed for a brief verbal report on the key points from each group's deliberations, followed by whole group discussion of the points made and ideas shared as appropriate. For five groups there should be five minutes for the verbal report and another five for discussion.
- Careful note requires to be taken of all the issues and ideas emerging, especially ideas for new practices to be trialled. This note is particularly important for leaders (senior management teams, etc.) to ensure they can assess any resources needed and how best to support any follow-up activities.
- Finally, the facilitators should wind up the session with a recap of all the major discussion points and proposals. They must also prepare a short summary note of the proceedings as both a record for everyone involved and as a means of focusing follow-up discussion among participants and the school leadership team.

# References

AERA, APA and NCME (1999) *Standards for Educational and Psychological Testing.* American Educational Research Association, American Psychological Association and National Commission on Measurement in Education, Washington DC: American Psychological Association.

Alexander, R.J. (2004) *Towards Dialogic Teaching: Rethinking Classroom Talk.* Cambridge: Dialogos.

ARG (2002a) *Testing, Motivation and Learning.* Assessment Reform Group. Available online at www.assessment-reform-group.org

ARG (2002b) *Assessment for Learning: 10 Principles.* Assessment Reform Group. Available online at www.assessment-reform-group.org/

ARG (2005) *The Role of Teachers in the Assessment of Learning.* Assessment Reform Group. Available online at www.assessment-reform-group.org/publications.html

ARG (2006) *The Role of Teachers in the Assessment of Learning.* Assessment Reform Group. Available online at www.assessment-reform-group.org

Baker, E. (2007) *The End(s) of Assessment.* Presidential Speech, American Educational Research Association Annual Conference, Chicago. Available online at www.cmcgc.com/Media/Synch/270409/40/default.htm

BBC News (2007a) Education, Education, Education, BBC News, 14 May. Available online at www.news.bbc.co.uk/1/hi/education/6640347.stm

BBC News (2007b) Schools repeatedly testing pupils, BBC News, 10 May. Available online at news.bbc.co.uk/1/hi/education/6640347.stm

BBC News (2008) Appeals soar after Sats fiasco, BBC News, 18 December. Available online at www.news.bbc.co.uk/1/hi/education/7789487.stm

BBC News (2009) Teachers back a boycott of Sats, BBC News, 11 April. Available online at www.news.bbc.co.uk/1/hi/education/7994882.stm

Benaby, A. (2006) Losing a year and gaining . . . nothing, *The Guardian*, 10 October.

Bergan, J.R., Sladeczek, I.E., Schwarz, R.D. and Smith, A.N. (1991) Effects of a measurement and planning system on kindergarteners' cognitive development and educational programming, *American Educational Research Journal*, 28: 683–714.

Black, C., Chan, V., MacLardie, J. and Murray, L. (2009) *Research on the Consultation on the Next Generation of National Qualifications in Scotland*. Scottish Government. Available online at www.scotland.gov.uk/Publications/2009/02/23130007/0

Black, P. (2001) Dreams, strategies and systems: portraits of assessment past, present and future, *Assessment in Education*, 8(1): 65–85.

Black, P. (1993) Formative and summative assessment by teachers, *Studies in Science Education*, 21: 49–97.

Black, P. (2008) Unpublished input to an Assessment Systems of the Future seminar, Cardiff, September.

Black, P., Harrison, C., Hodgen, J., Marshall, B. and Serret, N. (2006a) Strengthening teacher assessment practices, learning and evidence. Paper presented at the BERA Conference, University of Warwick, 6–8 September. See also www.kcl.ac.uk/schools/sspp/education/research/projects/kosap.html

Black, P., Harrison, C., Hodgen, J., Marshall, B. and Wiliam, D. (2005a) The dissemination of formative assessment: a lesson from, or about, evaluation, *Research Intelligence*, 92: 14–15.

Black, P., Harrison, C., Hodgen, J., Marshall, B. and Wiliam, D. (2005b) Dissemination and evaluation: a response to Smith and Gorard, *Research Intelligence*, 93: 7.

Black, P., McCormick, R., James, M. and Pedder, D. (2006b) Learning how to learn and assessment for learning: a theoretical inquiry, *Research Papers in Education*, 21(2): 119–32.

Black, P. and Wiliam, D. (1998a) Assessment and classroom learning, *Assessment in Education*, 5(1): 7–74.

Black, P. and Wiliam, D. (1998b) *Inside the Black Box*. Slough: NFER-Nelson.

Black, P. and Wiliam, D. (2002) *Standards in Public Examinations*. London: King's College, School of Education.

Black, P. and Wiliam, D. (2003) In praise of educational research: formative assessment, *British Educational Research Journal*, 29(5): 623–7.

Black, P. and Wiliam, D. (2006) The reliability of assessments, in J. Gardner (ed.) *Assessment and Learning*, pp. 119–31. London: Sage Publications.

Black, P.J., Harrison, C., Lee, C., Marshall, B. and Wiliam, D. (2002) *Working Inside the Black Box*. Slough: NFER-Nelson.

Black, P.J., Harrison, C., Lee, C., Marshall, B. and Wiliam, D. (2003) *Assessment for Learning: Putting it into Practice*. Maidenhead: Open University Press.

Blanchard, J., Collins, F., and Thorp, J. (2004) *Developing Assessment for Learning in Portsmouth City Primary Schools 2003–2004*. Portsmouth: Dame Judith Professional Development Centre, Cosham.

Boud, D. and Falchikov, N. (2007) (eds) *Rethinking Assessment in Higher Education: Learning for the Longer Term*. London: Routledge.

Bransford, J.D., Brown, A.L. and Cocking, R.R. (eds) (1999) *How People Learn: Brain, Mind, Experience and School*. Washington, DC: National Academy Press.

Brooks, S. and Tough, S. (2006) *Assessment and Testing: Making Space for Teaching and Learning*. Institute of Public Policy Research, London: IPPR.

Brousseau, G. (1984) The crucial role of the didactical contract in the analysis and construction of situations in teaching and learning mathematics, in H.G. Steiner (ed.) *Theory of Mathematics Education*, pp. 110–19. Paper presented at the ICME 5 Topic and Miniconference, Bielefeld, Germany: Institut fur Didaktik der Mathematik ber Universitat Bielefeld.

Brown, A.L. and Campione, J.C. (1996) Psychological theory and the design of innovative learning environments: on procedures, principles and systems, in L. Schauble and R. Glaser (eds) *Innovations in Learning: New Environments for Education*, pp. 289–325. New Jersey: Erlbaum.

Bruner, J. (1996) *The Culture of Education*. Cambridge, MA: Harvard University Press.

Bryan, C. and Clegg, K. (2006) *Innovative Assessment in Higher Education*. London: Routledge.

Burns, S. (2006) Developing AfL, monitoring progress and evaluating impact – a case study. Paper presented to the Assessment for School and Pupil Improvement conference, London, 27 June.

Butler, R. (1988) Enhancing and undermining intrinsic motivation: the effects of task-involving and ego-involving evaluation on interest and performance, *British Journal of Education Psychology*, 58: 1–14.

CCEA (2006) *Assessment for Learning Report*. Belfast: Council for the Curriculum, Examinations and Assessment.

CCEA (2009a) *Northern Ireland Curriculum*, Council for Curriculum, Examinations and Assessment. Available online at www.nicurriculum. org.uk/connected_learning/index.asp

CCEA (2009b) *Skills and Capabilities*, Council for Curriculum, Examinations and Assessment. Available online at www.nicurriculum. org.uk/skills_and_capabilities/index.asp

CCEA (2009c) *Assessing Thinking Skills and Personal Capabilities*, Council for Curriculum, Examinations and Assessment. Available online at www.nicurriculum.org.uk/key_stage_3/assessment_and_reporting/ thinking_skills_personal_capabilities.asp

CCEA (2009d) *Assessment for Learning*, Council for Curriculum, Examinations and Assessment. Available online at www.nicurriculum.org.uk/ assessment_for_learning/index.asp

CCEA (2009e) *Cross Curricular Skills at KS3*, Council for Curriculum, Examinations and Assessment. Available online at www.nicurriculum.org.uk/key_stage_3/assessment_and_reporting/cross_curricular_skills.asp

CCEA (2009f) *Cross Curricular Skills at KS3*, Council for Curriculum, Examinations and Assessment. Available online at www.nicurriculum.org.uk/key_stage_3/assessment_and_reporting/cross_curricular_skills.asp

CCEA (2009g) *InCAS and the Annual Report*, Council for Curriculum, Examinations and Assessment. Available online at www.nicurriculum.org.uk/annual_report/

CCEA (2009h) *Annual Report FS, KS1-2*, Northern Ireland Curriculum. Available online at www.nicurriculum.org.uk/key_stage_3/assessment_and_reporting/annual_report.asp

CIEA (2009) Government report recommends Chartered Educational Assessors in all schools, Chartered Institute of Educational Assessors. Available online at www.ciea.org.uk/news_and_events/press_releases/expert_panel_on_assessment.aspx

Clarke, S. (2003) *Enriching Feedback in the Primary Classroom and Formative Assessment in the Secondary Classroom*. London: Hodder & Stoughton.

Collins, S., Reiss, M. and Stobart, G. (2008) The effects of national testing in science at KS2 in England and Wales. Report to the Wellcome Trust, Institute of Education, University of London.

Colwill, I. (2007) *Improving GCSE Internal and Controlled Assessments*. Office of the Qualifications and Examinations Regulator. Available online at www.ofqual.gov.uk/files/qca-07-3207_Improving_GCSE_internal_and_controlled_assessment.pdf

Condie, R., Livingston, K. and Seagraves, L. (2005) *The Assessment Is for Learning Programme: Final Report*. Learning and Teaching Scotland. Available online at www.ltscotland.org.uk/publications/e/publication_tcm4509472.asp?strReferringChannel=assess

Conlon, T. (2004) A failure of delivery: the United Kingdom's New Opportunities Fund programme of teacher training in information and communications technology, *Journal of In-Service Education*, 30(1): 115–31.

Connected (2006) *Moving Education Forward*, Issue 16. Glasgow: Learning and Teaching Scotland.

Cooper, P. and McIntyre, D. (1996) *Effective Teaching and Learning: Teachers' and Students' Perspectives*. Maidenhead: Open University Press.

Crooks, T.J. (1988) The impact of classroom evaluation practices on students, *Review of Educational Research*, 58: 438–81.

Crossouard, B. and Sebba, J. (2006) An Evaluation of the AfL Initiatives in Jersey: *Final Report*. Sussex Institute, University of Sussex.

Cuban, L. (1994) *How Teachers Taught: Constancy and Change in American Classrooms 1890–1980*. New York: Teachers College Press.

Cullingford, C (2004) The future: is sustainability sustainable? In J. Blewitt and C. Cullingford (eds) *The Sustainability Curriculum*. London: Earthscan.

Daugherty, R. (2009) National curriculum assessment for learning: development programme, *Educational Research*, 51(2): 247–50.

DCELLS (2007) *Future Assessment Arrangements for Key Stages 2 and 3 – Report on the Findings and Outcomes of the National Consultation, Held 31 October 2006 to 12 January 2007*, Department for Children, Education, Lifelong Learning and Skills, Welsh Assembly Government. Available online at www.wales.gov.uk/docrepos/40382/4038232/403829/Consultations/870830/future-assesment-ks2ks3-report-e?lang=en

DCELLS (2008a) *Skills Framework for 3–19 year-olds in Wales*, Department for Children, Education, Lifelong Learning and Skills, Welsh Assembly Government. Available online at www.new.wales.gov.uk/dcells/publications/curriculum_and_assessment/arevisedcurriculumforwales/skillsdevelopment/SKILLS_FRAMEWORK_2007_Engli1.pdf;jsessionid=FPbSKQ0PlBJCyC1xDnl0yVxHtqhr2fZpprJFqZ9blt5yvdpgJwyY!-1059239472?lang=en

DCELLS (2008b) *Making the Most of Learning: Implementing the Revised Curriculum*, Department for Children, Education, Lifelong Learning and Skills, Welsh Assembly Government. Available online at www.new.wales.gov.uk/dcells/publications/curriculum_and_assessment/arevisedcurriculumforwales/nationalcurriculum/makingthemostoflearningnc/Making_Standard_WEB_(E).pdf?lang=en

DCELLS (2008c) *English in the National Curriculum for Wales*, Department for Children, Education, Lifelong Learning and Skills, Welsh Assembly Government. Available online at www.new.wales.gov.uk/dcells/publications/curriculum_and_assessment/arevisedcurriculumforwales/nationalcurriculum/englishnc/englishncoeng.pdf?lang=en

DCELLS (2008d) *Statutory Assessment and Reporting Arrangements for 2008: Primary*, Department for Children, Education, Lifelong Learning and Skills, Welsh Assembly Government. Available online at www.old.accac.org.uk/uploads/documents/2699.pdf

DCELLS (2008e) *Statutory Assessment Arrangements for School Year 2008–09: Key Stage 3*, Department for Children, Education, Lifelong Learning and Skills, Welsh Assembly Government. Available online at www.old.accac.org.uk/uploads/documents/2833.pdf

DCELLS (2008f) *Ensuring Consistency in Teacher Assessment: Guidance for Key Stages 2 and 3*, Department for Children, Education, Lifelong Learning and Skills, Welsh Assembly Government. Available online at www.wales.gov.uk/docrepos/40382/4038232/403829/4038293/1902288/teacherassessment;jsessionid=8XdTKTRGz9C1vhpRD6spGwGDR11lmfCLLF7LRcLwyHgJZ1Mc99Z0!-1059239472?lang=en

DCELLS (2009a) *Developing Thinking and Assessment for Learning: Development Programme*. Department for Children, Education, Lifelong Learning and Skills, Welsh Assembly Government. Available online at www.new.wales.gov.uk/topics/educationandskills/curriculumassessment/thinkingandassessmentforlearning/?lang=en

DCELLS (2009b) *Work Based Learning Pathways – Guide for Parents and Guardians*, Welsh Assembly Government. Available online at www.wales.gov.uk/docs/dcells/publications/090303wblpparentsen.pdf

DCSF (2008a) *The Assessment for Learning Strategy*, Department for Children, Schools and Families. Available online at www.publications.teachernet.gov.uk/default.aspx?PageFunction=productdetails&PageMode=publications&ProductId=DCSF-00341-2008

DCSF (2008b) *Press Release 2008/0229, Major Reforms to Schools Accountability*. Department for Children, Schools and Families. Available online at www.dcsf.gov.uk/pns/DisplayPN.cgi?pn_id=2008_0229

DCSF (2008c) *Ed Balls Announces New 'Schools Report Cards'*, Department for Children, Schools and Families. Available online at www.dcsf.gov.uk/pns/DisplayPN.cgi?pn_id=2008_0229

DCSF (2009a) *New Focus Area for Assessment of Pupil Progress*, Department for Children Schools and Families. Available online at www.nationalstrategies.standards.dcsf.gov.uk/secondary

DCSF (2009b) *Press Release 2009/0090, Ed Balls' Response to the Expert Group on Assessment*, Department for Children Schools and Families. Available online at www.dcsf.gov.uk/pns/DisplayPN.cgi?pn_id=2009_0090

DCSF (2009c) *Report of the Expert Group on Assessment*, Department for Children Schools and Families. Available online at www.publications.dcsf.gov.uk/eOrderingDownload/Expert-Group-Report.pdf

DCSF (2009d) *The National Strategies*, Department for Children, Schools and Families. Available online at www.nationalstrategies.standards.dcsf.gov.uk/

DE (2008) *Consultation on Draft Regulations to Specify Requirements Relating to the Reporting of Pupil Information to Parents and the Keeping, Disclosure and Transfer of Pupil Records*, Department of Education for Northern Ireland. Available online at www.deni.gov.uk/consultation_doc.pdf

DE (2006) *Pupil Profile and Changes to Statutory Assessment – Post Primary*, Department of Education for Northern Ireland. Available online at www.deni.gov.uk/pupil-profile-and-changes-to-statutory-assessment-post-primary-3.pdf

DENI (1996) *The Northern Ireland Curriculum Key Stages 1 and 2: Programmes of Study and Attainment Targets*. Department of Education for Northern Ireland. Befast: HMSO. Available online at www.deni.gov.uk/index/80-curriculum-and-assessment/80-programmes-of-study-htm

DES/WO (1988) *National Curriculum: Task Group on Assessment and Testing. A Report.* London: The Stationery Office.

Dewey, J. (1938) *Experience and Education.* New York: Simon & Schuster.

Drakeford, M. (2007) Progressive universalism, *Agenda,* Winter: 4–7.

Elliott, J. (ed.) (1993) *Reconstructing Teacher Education: Teacher Development.* London: Falmer Press.

Embretson, S.E. (2003) *The Second Century of Ability Testing: Some Predictions and Speculations.* Princeton, NJ: Educational Testing Service.

Fitch, J. (1898) *Lectures on Teaching.* Cambridge: Cambridge University Press, 158–9 (lectures first given in 1880).

Flexer, R.J., Cumbo, K., Borko, H., Mayfield, V. and Maion, S.F. (1995) *How 'Messing About' with Performance Assessment in Mathematics Affects What Happens in Classrooms, Technical Report 396.* Los Angeles Centre for Research on Evaluation, Standards and Student Testing (CRESST), University of California, Los Angeles.

Foxman, D., Hutchinson, D. and Bloomfield, B. (1991) *The APU Experience, 1977–1990.* London: Schools Examination and Assessment Council.

Frederiksen, J. and White, B. (1994) Mental models and understanding: a problem for science education, in E. Scanlon and T. O'Shea (eds) *New Directions in Educational Technology.* New York: Springer-Verlag.

Fuchs, L.S. and Fuchs, D. (1986) Effects of systematic formative evaluation: a meta-analysis, *Exceptional Children,* 53: 199–208.

Fullan, M. (1993) *Change Forces: Probing the Depths of Educational Reform.* London: Falmer Press.

Fullan, M. (2003) *Change Forces with a Vengeance.* London: Routledge-Falmer.

Fullan, M. (2004) *Systems Thinkers in Action: Moving Beyond the Standards Plateau.* Innovation Unit, Department for Education and Skills, London: DfES. Available online at www.innovation-unit.co.uk/images/stories/files/pdf/SystemsThinkersinAction.pdf

Galanouli, D., Murphy, C. and Gardner, J. (2004) Teachers' perceptions of the effectiveness of ICT-competence training, *Computers and Education,* 43(1–2): 63–79.

Gardner, J. (2007) Is teaching a partial profession? In *Make the Grade,* 18–22, Summer Issue. London: Chartered Institute of Educational Assessors.

Gardner, J. and Cowan, P. (2005) The fallibility of high stakes '11 plus' testing in Northern Ireland, *Assessment in Education,* 12(2): 145–65.

Gipps, C. (1994) *Beyond Testing.* London: Falmer Press.

Gordon, S. and Reese, M. (1997) High stakes testing: worth the price? *Journal of School Leadership,* 7: 345–68.

Green, T.F. (1998) *The Activities of Teaching.* Troy, NY: Educator's International Press.

Hall, K. and Harding, A. (2002) Level descriptions and teacher assessment in England: towards a community of assessment practice, *Educational Research,* 44: 1–15.

Hall, K., Webber, B., Varley, S., Young, V. and Dorman, P. (1997) A study of teachers' assessment at Key Stage 1, *Cambridge Journal of Education,* 27: 107–22.

Hargreaves, D. (2005) *About Learning: Report of the Learning Working Group.* London: Demos.

Harlen, W. (2004) Trusting teachers' judgments: research evidence of the reliability and validity of teachers' assessment used for summative purposes, *Research Papers in Education,* 20(3): 245–70.

Harlen, W. (2006) On the relationship between assessment for formative and summative purposes, in J. Gardner (ed.) *Assessment and Learning,* pp. 103–17. London: Sage Publications.

Harlen, W. (2007) *Assessment of Learning.* London: Sage Publications.

Harlen, W. and Deakin Crick, R. (2002) *A Systematic Review of the Impact of Summative Assessment and Tests on Students' Motivation for Learning.* Research Evidence in Education Library, Evidence for Policy and Practice Information Coordinating Centre (EPPI Centre), Social Science Research Unit, London: Institute of Education. Available online at www.eppi.ioe.ac.uk/cms/Default.aspx?tabid=108

Harlen, W. and Deakin Crick, R.W. (2003) Testing and motivation for learning, *Assessment in Education,* 10(2): 169–207

Harlen, W. and James, M. (1997) Assessment and learning: differences and relationships between formative and summative assessment, *Assessment in Education,* 4(3): 365–80.

Hattie, J. (2003) *Teachers make a difference: what is the research evidence?* Australian Council for Educational Research Annual Conference on Building Teacher Quality, Melbourne, October. Available online at www.education.auckland.ac.nz/webdav/site/education/shared/hattie/docs/teachers-make-a-difference-ACER-(2003).pdf

Hayward, L., Priestly, M. and Young, M. (2004) Ruffling the calm of the ocean floor: merging research, policy and practice in Scotland, *Oxford Review of Education,* 30(3): 397–415.

Hayward, L. and Spencer, E. (2006) There is no alternative to trusting teachers, in M. Sainsbury, C. Harrison, and A. Watts (eds) *Assessing Reading – From Theories to Classrooms,* pp. 222–40. Slough: NFER.

Hayward, L., Spencer, E. and Simpson, M. (2005) *Exploring Programme Success, Assessment is for Learning: Report to Scottish Government.* Glasgow: Learning and Teaching Scotland. Available online at www.ltscotland.org.uk/Images/AifL%20Exploring%20Programme%20Success_tcm4-354151.pdf

HEFCW (2009) *Credit and Qualifications Framework for Wales.* Higher Education Funding Council for Wales. Available online at www.hefcw.ac.uk/ Learning_and_Teaching/framework.htm

Hilliam A., Granville, S. and Costley, N. (2007) *Evaluation of Assessment Of Learning: Final Report.* Learning and Teaching Scotland. Available online at www.ltscotland.org.uk/Images/5419%20AoL%20Final%20Report%20v3_tcm4-471962.pdf

HMI (1999) *Review of Assessment in Pre-school and 5–14.* Her Majesty's Inspectors of Schools, Edinburgh: HMSO.

HMIE (2006a) *How Good is Our School? The Journey to Excellence.* Her Majesty's Inspectorate of Education, Edinburgh: HMIE. Available online at www.hmie.gov.uk/documents/publication/hgiosjte.pdf

HMIE (2006b) *Improving Scottish Education: A Report by HMIE on Inspection and Review 2002–2005.* Her Majesty's Inspectorate of Education, Edinburgh: HMIE.

Hodgen, J. and Marshall, B. (2005) Assessment for learning in English and mathematics: a comparison, *The Curriculum Journal*, 16(2): 153–76.

Holmes, B., Gardner, J. and Galanouli, D. (2007) Striking the right chord and sustaining successful professional development in ICT, *Journal of In-Service Education*, 33(4): 389–404.

Hutchinson, C. and Hayward, L. (2005) Assessment in Scotland: the journey so far, *Curriculum Journal*, 16(2): 225–48.

IEA (2009) *Trends in International Mathematics and Science Study.* International Association for the Evaluation of Educational Achievement, Amsterdam: IEA. Available online at www.iea.nl/

Illinois (2007) *Performance Standard 24B.E.* Illinois State Education Board. Available online at www.isbe.state.il.us/ils/pdh/health/stage_E/24BE.pdf

James, M. and Brown, S. (2005) Grasping the TLRP nettle: preliminary analysis and some enduring issues surrounding the improvement of learning outcomes, *The Curriculum Journal*, 16(1): 7–30.

James, M. and Pedder, D. (2006) Professional learning as a condition for Assessment for Learning, in J. Gardner (ed.) *Assessment and Learning*, pp. 27–43. London: Sage Publications.

James, M., Black, P., McCormick, R., Pedder, D. and Wiliam, D. (2006a) Learning how to learn in classrooms, schools and networks: aims, design and analysis, *Research Papers in Education*, 21(2): 101–18.

James, M., Black, P., Carmichael, P., Conner, C., Dudley, P., Fox, A., Frost, D., Honour, L., MacBeath, J., McCormick, R., Marshall, B., Pedder, D., Procter, R., Swaffield, S. and Wiliam, D. (2006b) *Learning How to Learn: Tools for Schools.* TLRP Improving Practice Series, London: Routledge.

Jones, K. and Alexiadou, N. (2001) The global and the national: reflections on the experience of three European states. Paper presented at the *European Conference on Educational Research*, Lille, 5–8 September.

Kellaghan, T. (1996) IEA studies and educational policy, *Assessment in Education*, 3(2): 143–60.

Kellard, K., Costello, M., Godfrey, D., Griffiths, E. and Rees, C. (2008) *Evaluation of the Developing Thinking and Assessment for Learning Development Programme*. Department for Children, Education, Lifelong Learning and Skills, Cardiff: Welsh Assembly Government. Available online at www.wales.gov.uk/docs/dcells/publications/090218evalutationreporten.pdf

King's College (2009) *King's Oxfordshire Summative Assessment Project (KOSAP)*. Available online at www.kcl.ac.uk/schools/sspp/education/research/projects/kosap.html

Kirkwood, M., van der Kuyl, T., Parton, N. and Grant, R. (2000) The New Opportunities Fund (NOF) ICT Training for Teachers Programme: designing a powerful on-line learning environment. Paper presented at the *European Conference on Educational Research*, Edinburgh, 20–23 September. Available online at www.leeds.ac.uk/educol/documents/00001690.htm

Kirton, A., Hallam, S., Peffers, J., Robertson, P. and Stobart, G. (2007) Revolution, evolution or a Trojan horse? Piloting assessment for learning in some Scottish primary schools, *British Educational Research Journal*, 33(4): 605–27.

Kulik, C-L. C. and Kulik, J.A. (1987) Mastery testing and student learning: a meta-analysis, *Journal of Educational Technology Systems*, 15: 325–45.

Lave, J. and Wenger, E. (1991) *Situated Learning: Legitimate Peripheral Participation*. New York: Cambridge University Press.

Leitch, R., Gardner, J., Mitchell, S., Lundy, L., Clough, P., Galanouli, D. and Odena, O. (2006) Researching creatively with pupils in Assessment for Learning (AfL) classrooms on experiences of participation and consultation. Paper presented at the *European Conference on Educational Research*, University of Geneva, September. Available online at www.leeds.ac.uk/educol/documents/157844.htm

LHTL (2009) *Learning How to Learn Project*. Available online at www.learntolearn.ac.uk

LTS (2009a) *Scottish Survey of Achievement*. Learning and Teaching Scotland. Available online at www.ltscotland.org.uk/assess/of/ssa/index.asp

LTS (2009b) *AifL: Assessment is for Learning*. Learning and Teaching Scotland. Available online at www.ltscotland.org.uk/assess/index.asp

Mansell, W. (2007) *Education by Numbers: The Tyranny of Testing*. London: Politico's.

Marshall, B. and Drummond, M.J. (2006) How teachers engage with Assessment for Learning: lessons from the classroom, *Research Papers in Education*, 21(2): 133–50.

Maxwell, G.S. (2004) Progressive assessment for learning and certification: some lessons from school-based assessment in Queensland. Paper presented at the *Third Conference of the Association of Commonwealth Examination and Assessment Boards*, 'Redefining the Roles of Educational Assessment', March, Nadi, Fiji.

Messick, S. (1989) Validity, in R.L. Linn (ed.) *Educational Measurement*, 3rd edn., pp. 12–103. London: Collier Macmillan.

Morrish, I. (1976) *Aspects of Educational Change*. London: George Allen & Unwin.

NAfW (2001) *The Learning Country: A Comprehensive Education and Lifelong Learning Programme to 2010 for Wales*. Cardiff: National Assembly for Wales.

NAS/UWT (2008) *Testing to Destruction* NAS/UWT. Available online at www.nasuwt.org.uk/index.htm

NAS/UWT (2009) *The Root of the Problem is not Sats*. NAS/UWT Press Release. Available online at www.nasuwt.org.uk/Whatsnew/NASUWTNews/PressReleases/TherootoftheproblemisnotSATsitsthecurrentaccountabilityregimesaystheNASUWT/NASUWT_004103

Natriello, G. (1987) The impact of evaluation processes on students, *Educational Psychologist*, 22: 155–75.

Newton, P.E. (2007) Clarifying the purposes of educational assessment, *Assessment and Education: Principles, Policy and Practice*, 14(2): 149–70.

Newton, P.E. (2009) Recognising the error of our ways. The reliability of results from national curriculum testing in England, *Cambridge Educational Research*, 51(2): 181–212.

NUT (2006) *The Impact of National Curriculum Testing on Pupils*. National Union of Teachers Briefing, September 2006.

NUT/NAHT (2009) *NUT/NAHT Joint Statement on Sats*. March 2009, National Union of Teachers. Available online at www.teachers.org.uk/story.php?id=4654

OECD (2005) *Formative Assessment: Improving Learning in Secondary Classrooms*. Organization for Economic Co-operation and Development, Paris: OECD.

OECD (2009) *Programme for International Student Achievement*. Organization for Economic Co-operation and Development. Paris: OECD. Available online at www.pisa.oecd.org/pages/0,2987,en_32252351_32235731_1_1_1_1_1,00.html

OFSTED (2002) *ICT in Schools: Effect of Government Initiatives – Pupils' Achievement – Progress Report*. London: The Stationery Office.

OFSTED (2004) *ICT in Schools: The Impact of Government Initiatives Five Years On*. London: The Stationery Office. Available online at www.ofsted.gov.uk/Ofsted-home/Publications-and-research/Browse-all-by/Education/Curriculum/Information-and-communication-technology/Primary/ICT-in-schools-2004-theimpact-of-government-initiatives-five-years-on

Ozga, J. and Jones, R. (2006) Travelling and embedded policy: the case of knowledge transfer, *Journal of Education Policy*, 21(1): 1–17.

Pressey, S.L. (1926) A simple apparatus which gives tests and scores – and teaches, *School and Society*, 23(586): 373–6.

Preston, C. (2004) *Learning to use ICT in Classrooms: Teachers' and Trainers' Perspectives*. London: TTA/MirandaNet. Available online at www.mirandanet.ac.uk/tta/

QCA (2005) *A Review of GCE and GCSE Coursework Arrangements*. Qualifications and Curriculum Authority. Available online at www.qca.org.uk/libraryAssets/media/qca-05-1845-coursework-report.pdf

QCA (2006a) *Authenticating Coursework*. Office of the Qualifications and Examinations Regulator. Available online at www.ofqual.gov.uk/files/qca-06-2377-coursework-t.pdf

QCA (2006b) *Monitoring Pupils' Progress in English at KS3. Final Report on the 2003–05 Pilot*. Qualifications and Curriculum Authority, London: QCA.

QCA (2007a) *Personal Learning and Thinking Skills Framework*. Qualifications and Curriculum Authority. London: QCA. Available online at www.qca.org.uk/qca_5866.aspx

QCA (2007b) *Evaluation of the Monitoring Children's Progress Pilot Project*. Qualifications and Curriculum Authority. London: QCA. Available online at www.qcda.org.uk/libraryAssets/media/third_interim.pdf

QCA (2008a) *GCSE Controlled Assessment Regulations*. Qualifications and Curriculum Authority. Available online at www.qca.org.uk/libraryAssets/media/GCSE_Controlled_Assessment_Regulations_February_2008_QCA-08-3512.pdf

QCA (2008b) *Early Years Foundation Stage*. Qualifications and Curriculum Authority. Available online at www.qca.org.uk/qca_13585.aspx

QCA (2009) *Teacher Assessment and Reporting Arrangements Key Stage 3 2009*. Qualifications and Curriculum Authority. Available online at www.testsandexams.qca.org.uk/21417.aspx

QCDA (2009a) *Assessment and Reporting Arrangements Key Stage 1 ARA*. London: QCDA. Available online at www.testsandexams.qcda.gov.uk/19527.aspx

QCDA (2009b) *Assessment*. London: QCDA. Available online at www.qcda.gov.uk/13581.aspx

Reay, D. and Wiliam, D. (1999) 'I'll be a nothing': structure, agency and the construction of identity through assessment, *British Educational Research Journal*, 25: 343–5.

Reeves, J. (2007) Inventing the chartered teacher, *British Journal of Educational Studies*, 55(1): 56–76.

Richardson, T. (2005) *States of Jersey: Assessment at Key Stages One and Two. Evaluation of the Effectiveness of Teacher Assessments.* SERCO Learning Consultancy. Available online at www.antiochne.edu/acsr/criticalskills/TeacherAssessmentReport.pdf

Rogers, E.M. (1962) *Diffusion of Innovations*. New York: The Free Press.

Rogers, E.M. (1983) *Diffusion of Innovations, 3rd edn.* New York: The Free Press.

Rose, J. (2009) *Independent Review of the Primary Curriculum: Final Report.* Teachernet, Department for Children, Schools and Families. Available online at www.publications.teachernet.gov.uk/eOrderingDownload/Primary_curriculum_Report.pdf

Rudduck, J. (1976) *Dissemination of Innovation: The Humanities Curriculum Project.* Schools Council Working Paper 56. London: Evans/Methuen.

Rudduck, J. and Kelly, P. (1976) *The Dissemination of Curriculum Development: Current Trends.* Slough: NFER.

Sadler, D.R. (1989) Formative assessment and the design of instructional systems, *Instructional Science*, 18: 119–44.

Sarason, S. (1971) *The Culture of the School and the Problem of Change.* Boston, MA: Allyn & Bacon.

Schön, D. (1971) *Beyond the Stable State*. London: Temple Smith.

Schön, D. (1983) *The Reflective Practitioner.* Aldershot: Ashgate Publishing.

Schunk, D. (1996) Goal and self-evaluative influences during children's cognitive skill learning, *American Educational Research Journal*, 33: 359–82.

Schwartzman, H.B. (1993) What happened at Hawthorne?, in H.B. Schwartzman, *Ethnography in Organizations*, pp. 5–26. London: Sage Publications.

Scottish Government (2005) *Scottish Survey of Achievement Information Sheet.* Publications, Scottish Government. Available online at www.scotland.gov.uk/Publications/2005/09/20105646/56474

Scottish Government (2008a) *Next Generation of Qualifications.* News, Scottish Government. Available online at www.scotland.gov.uk/News/Releases/2008/12/02124242

Scottish Government (2008b) *Maths and Science League Tables.* News, Scottish Government. Available online at www.scotland.gov.uk/News/Releases/2008/12/09163549

Scottish Government (2009) *New Curriculum Must be Rigorously Assessed.* News, Scottish Government. Available online at www.scotland.gov.uk/News/Releases/2009/02/27110626

SD (2005) *One Future – Different Paths*. Sustainable Development Agency. Available online at www.sd-commission.org.uk/publications.php?id=215

SEED (2005) *Information Sheet on the Scottish Survey of Achievement*. Scottish Executive Education Department, Edinburgh: SEED.

Senge, P. and Scharmer, O. (2001) Community action research: learning as a community of practitioners, in P. Reason and H. Bradbury (eds) *Handbook of Action Research: Participative Inquiry and Practice*, pp. 238–49. London: Sage Publications.

Senge, P., Scharmer, C.O., Jaworski, J. and Flowers, B.S. (2005). *Presence: Exploring Profound Change in People, Organizations and Society*. London: Nicholas Brearley Publishing.

Senge, P.M., Scharmer, C.O., Jaworski, J. and Flowers, B.S. (2004) *Presence: Human Purpose and the Field of Future*. Cambridge, MA: Society for Organizational Learning.

Sfard, A. (1998) On two metaphors for learning and the dangers of choosing just one, *Educational Researcher*, 27(2): 4–13.

Skidmore, P. (2003) *Beyond Measure: Why Educational Assessment is Failing the Test*. London: Demos.

Smith, E. and Gorard, S. (2005) 'They don't give us our marks': the role of formative feedback in student progress, *Assessment in Education*, 12(1): 21–38.

SOED (1991) *Curriculum and Assessment in Scotland. Assessment 5–14 – Improving the Quality of Learning and Teaching*. Scottish Office Education Department, Edinburgh: HMSO.

SOEID (1992) *Reporting 5–14: Improving Partnership with Parents*. Scottish Office Education and Industry Department, Edinburgh: HMSO.

SQA (2009a) *National Assessment Bank Materials*. Scottish Qualifications Authority. Available online at www.sqa.org.uk/sqa/4739.html

SQA (2009b) *Scottish Baccalaureates*. Scottish Qualifications Authority. Available online at www.sqa.org.uk/sqa/33765.html

Stobart, G. and Stoll, L. (2005) The Key Stage 3 Strategy: what kind of reform is this? *Cambridge Journal of Education*, 35(2): 225–38.

Stoll, L. and Fink, D. (1996) *Changing Our Schools: Linking School Effectiveness and School Improvement*. Buckingham: Open University Press.

Swaffield, S. and MacBeath, J. (2006) Embedding learning: how to learn in school policy: the challenge for leadership, *Research Papers in Education*, 21(2): 201–15.

TESS (2008) City council says Scottish Survey of Achievement fails to provide valid information, *Times Educational Supplement* (Scotland), September, p. 5.

The Times (2008) Ed Balls refuses to intervene over marking debacle, July, 22. Available online at www.timesonline.co.uk/tol/news/uk/article4379395.ece

Tymms, P. (2004) Are standards rising in English primary schools? *British Educational Research Journal*, 30: 477–94.

Way, W.D., Davis, L.L. and Fitzpatrick, S. (2006) *Practical Questions in Introducing Computerized Adaptive Testing for K-12 Assessments. Research Report 05-03.* Pearson Educational Measurement. Available online at www.pearsonedmeasurement.com/downloads/research/RR_05_03.pdf

White, B.Y. and Frederiksen, J.T. (1998) Inquiry, modeling and metacognition: making science accessible to all students, *Cognition and Instruction*, 16(1): 3–118.

Wiliam, D. (2001) Reliability, validity and all that jazz, *Education 3–13*, 29(3): 17–21.

Wiliam, D., Lee, C., Harrison, C. and Black, P. (2004) Teachers developing assessment for learning: impact on student achievement, *Assessment in Education*, 11(1): 49–66.

Wise, S.L. and Kingsbury, G.G. (2000) Practical issues in developing and maintaining a computerized adaptive testing program, *Psicológica*, 21: 135–55.

# Index

access to tasks 66–7
accountability
    and agency 131
    Key Stage (SATs) tests 55, 56
    and monitoring pupil achievement
        16, 17–18, 65
    school inspectors 168
    and sustainability 169–70
accuracy/error 37, 44, 77
    principle of assessment practice
        38–9
acquisition *vs* participation metaphors
    of learning 133
adaptive tests, computerized (CATs)
    77–8
administration, innovation in 76–8
AfL *see* assessment for learning
agency 130–1
    and advocacy 145
    conceptions of 131–2
    counterproductive 137
    elements of readiness 134–7
    as key to change 133–4
    'top-down' and 'bottom-up' models
        132–3
Alexander, R.J. 35
ARIA study 7–8, 46–7, 172–3 *appendix*
    agency 134, 136
    evaluation of innovation 142, 144,
        145, 146, 152, 153
    professional learning 124, 126–7,
        128
    sustainability 170
    *see also* principles of assessment
        practice
Assessment is for Learning Programme
    (AifL), Scotland 66, 93–4, 117,
        135, 150, 166–7
assessment for learning (AfL) 39, 40,
    54–5
    evaluation of innovation 142, 150,
        152
    professional learning 108–10, 111

teacher roles in 64–8
    *see also* formative assessment
*Assessment for Learning Strategy* (DCSF)
    54–5
Assessment of Pupil Progress
    (APP/QCA) 55, 163–4
Assessment Reform Group (ARG) 7, 32,
    41–2, 75, 111, 112, 160
    *The Role of Teachers in the Assessment
        of Learning* 64–8
attainments 143
    and control groups, pre-innovation
        147–50
attitudes
    changes in 146–7
    of pupils 143, 144, 146–7
'authentic assessment' 81
awareness
    and commitment 101–2
    raising 134–7

Balls, Ed 3, 55
baseline descriptors of pre-innovation
    practices and standards 145–50
Benaby, A. 17
'best fit' approach 27, 46
Black Box publications 21, 114, 117
Black, P. 96
    *et al.* 16, 21, 59, 63–4, 92–3, 107–8,
        134, 162–3, 166–7
    and Wiliam, D. 21, 23, 38, 73, 75,
        104, 105–6, 113–14, 134–5,
        166–7
Blanchard, J. et al. 108–9, 110, 111
Bransford, J.D. et al. 34, 104–5, 127
Brooks, S. and Tough, S. 27
Bruner, J. 96

cascade model of dissemination 89–90
CATs *see* computerized adaptive tests
CCEA *see* Council for Curriculum,
    Examinations and Assessment,
    Northern Ireland

change *see* agency; dissemination; innovation; professional learning; sustainability
Chartered Assessors (CIEA) 55, 56
citizenship education 34
Clarke, Shirely 108, 114, 115, 121
classroom-based teacher assessment 2
'collaborative' and 'individualistic' approaches 158–60
collaborative process of change 92–3
commitment and awareness 101–2
compliance, requirement for 137
communication technology (ICT) 73, 76–8, 132
computerized adaptive tests (CATs) 77–8
conditions for learning 35
Connected 86
control groups and attainment levels, pre-innovation 147–50
controlled tasks 163
Council for Curriculum, Examinations and Assessment (CCEA), Northern Ireland 60–1, 121, 165
counterproductive agency 137
coursework 81
critical thinking skills 113–14, 116
Crossouard, B. and Sebba, J. 114, 115, 116, 146
Cuban, L. 85
Cullingford, C. 155–6
*Curriculum for Excellence*, Scotland 58, 59, 64

Daugherty Report 58, 164–5
Department for Children, Education, Lifelong Learning and Skills (DCELLS), Wales 56, 57, 63, 117, 120, 146, 165–6
Department for Children, Schools and Families (DCSF) 54, 55, 122, 163–4
Department of Education, Northern Ireland 61
Department for Education and Skills (DfES) 122
descriptive studies 96
*Developing Thinking and Assessment for Learning: Development Programme* (DCELLS) 57

developmental criteria 64, 66
Dewey, J. 81–2
dialogical teaching 35
discussion and reflection 125–6
dissemination 85
and innovation 95–8
'top-down' and 'bottom-up' models 86
as tranformation 91–5
as transmission 86–91
domains of learning 42–3
Drakeford, M. 165

Early Years Foundation Stage Profile (EYFSP) 43, 54, 55, 160–1
Edisford Primary School study 151
effective learning
components of 96
sustainability of 157–8
embedded *vs* travelling policy 91
England 54–6, 62–3, 122–3
*see also* Key Stage assessments; King's College studies; national curriculum assessment
error *see* accuracy/error
evaluation of innovation 141–2
framework 145–52
methods and categories 142–5
evidence
formative assessment 20–1
of outcomes 151
and transparency 65, 66
triangulation of 144, 151
validity of 35–7, 82–3
examinations and education 3, 17, 79
external testing 3–4, 27, 80

facilitation and reporting of progress 33–5
feedback 18, 32, 36, 41
self-regulation and 170
for teachers 126
Fitch, J. 3
formative assessment
change in 165–8
effectiveness of 104, 145
Jersey project 113–16
KMOFAP project 105–8, 117, 118, 149–50
professional learning 118, 120
and regulation 170

supporting learning 19–22, 75
theory and practice 156
*see also* assessment for learning (AfL)
formative and summative assessment
6–7
*Assessment for Learning Strategy*
(DCSF) 54–5
linking 67
principles of assessment practice 31,
39–40
professional learning 123–4
standards for practice 48–51
supporting learning 16–19,
26–7
Foundation Stage Profile (EYFSP) 43,
54, 55, 160–1
full participation model (A) of
professional learning 103, 104,
106, 111, 113, 118, 125–6
Fullan, M. 73, 78–9, 85, 96, 130

General Certificate in Secondary
Education (GCSE) 2, 3, 62–3,
108, 161
Gipps, C. 16
graded assessment schemes 161–2

Hall, K. and Harding, A. 32, 158–9
Harlen, W. 22, 25–6, 32, 35–6
and Deakin Crick, R. 17, 22–3, 23–4,
31–2
and James, M. 142
Hayward, L.
et al. 59, 93–5, 117, 118–19, 150
and Spencer, E. 90–1, 95, 167
higher-order learning 143
Holmes, B. et al. 135–6

improving learning *see* supporting
learning
in-service days, Portsmouth project
108–9, 111
in-service professional development
64, 66
indifference 137
'individualistic' and 'collaborative'
approaches 158–60
information and communication
technology (ICT) 73, 76–8,
132
initiative overload 1

innovation 71–2
in assessment 74–6
types 76–83
and dissemination 95–8
lessons from 162–8
nature of 72–4
*see also* evaluation of innovation
interactive learning 27, 109
interpretations of outcomes 152

James, M.
and Brown, S. 96, 143, 144
et al. 23, 146
Harlen, W. and 142
and Pedder, D. 73
Jersey (King's College and JAFA
projects) 113–16, 146
'judgement', aspects of 82

Kellard, K. et al. 165–6
Key Stage 1 assessment 54, 55, 56, 61,
158–9
Key Stage 2 assessment 17, 38, 54, 55,
56, 61, 112–13, 120, 122, 164
Key Stage 3 assessment 54, 55, 56, 61,
89, 108, 120, 122–3, 163, 164
King's College studies
Black Box publications 21, 114, 117
Jersey formative assessment project
113–16
Medway Oxfordshire Formative
Assessment Project (KMOFAP)
105–8, 117, 118, 149–50
Oxfordshire Summative Use of
Assessment Project (KOSAP)
111–12, 127, 162–3

'league tables' 3, 17
'learning contract' 22
Learning How to Learn (LHTL) project
92–3, 146–7
learning roles 19–20, 39–40, 64–8
literacy, aspects of 33–4

marketing programme strategy of
dissemination 88
Marshall, B. and Drummond, J. 23
Maxwell, G.S. 26
misclassification of test results 37, 44
monitoring pupil achievement 16,
17–18, 65

*Monitoring Pupil Progress* (QCA) 146
Morrish, I. 76
motivation of students 40–2

NAS/UWT 54, 56, 57
national curriculum assessment
158–60
*see also* Key Stage assessments
national standards 17–18
negative effects of testing 17, 23–4,
31–2
and student motivation 40–2
'new learning', innovations for 80–3
Newton, P.E. 15
Northern Ireland 60–3, 121–2, 135, 165
novice-competent-expert continuum
126–7
Nuffield Foundation 7
NUT/NAHT 56

Ofqual 62
OFSTED 73
Ozga, J. and Jones, R. 91

participation
A & B models of professional
learning 103, 104, 106, 111–12,
113, 114–15, 118, 125–6
of students 18–19
*vs* acquisition metaphors of learning
133
performance targets 4, 17
'pilot and roll out' strategy of
dissemination 90
Portsmouth Learning Community:
Assessment for Learning Strand
108–11, 114, 119
potential of summative assessment
24–5
practice
extent and quality of 21–2
lessons from 168–9
pre-innovation 145–50
*vs* theory/principles 124–5, 133, 156
practice of techniques model (D) of
professional learning 103,
104–5, 110, 115, 123, 125
pre-innovation practices and standards
145–50
pre-service and in-service professional
development 64, 66

principles of assessment practice 30–44
and actual practice 124–5, 133, 156
professional development template
174–7
professional learning 100–1, 127–8
choice of approach 104
degrees of implementation of
change 101–2
examples in assessment reform
projects 105–16
lessons from 123–7
implementation at national level
117–23
models 102–5
public understanding of learning goals
37–8
pupil-focused approach 4–5
pupils/students
attitudes 143, 144, 146–7
feedback 18, 32, 36, 41
motivation 40–2
participation 18–19
relationship with teachers 22, 27,
35, 109
role in learning and assessment
39–40

qualifications 62–4
Qualifications and Curriculum
Authority (QCA) 74–5, 122,
123, 151
*A Review of GCE and GCSE
Coursework Arrangements* 62
Assessment of Pupil Progress (APP)
55, 163–4
*Monitoring Pupil Progress* 146
quality
robust and permanent procedures
64, 65–6
*see also* standards
questionnaire data 146–7

Reay, D. and Wiliam, D. 32, 41, 42
record sheets 163
reflection 74, 137
and discussion 125–6
regulation 170
resource-based models of
dissemination 87–9
*A Review of GCE and GCSE Coursework
Arrangements* (QCA) 62

robust and permanent procedures 64,
    65–6
*The Role of Teachers in the Assessment of
    Learning* (ARG) 64–8
rubric model 81–2
Ruddick, J. 72
    and Kelly, P. 101

sampling 67
SATs (standardized assessment task)
    *see* Key Stage assessments
saturation strategy of dissemination 87
scattergun model of dissemination
    86–7
Schön, D. 72, 74
school effectiveness indicators 67
school inspectors 168
school 'league tables' 3, 17
'School Report Card' 56
Scotland 58–60, 63–4
    AifL model 66, 93–4, 117, 135, 150,
        166–7
    *Curriculum for Excellence* 58, 59, 64
    dissemination models 87–8, 89,
        90–1, 91–2
    professional learning 117–20
    sustainability 166–8
selective dissemination strategy of
    dissemination 87
self-agency *see* agency
self-assessment, principle of
    assessment practice 42–3
self-selecting strategy of dissemination
    87–8
Senge, P.
    et al. 158
    and Scharmer, C.O. 93
sharing good practice strategy of
    dissemination 89
simulated participation model (B) of
    professional learning 103, 104,
        111–12, 113, 114–15, 118, 125
situated innovation 78–80
Skidmore, P. 80
Smith, E. and Gorard, S. 22, 151–2
special tasks 163
standards
    for classroom assessment practice
        47, 48–51
    'health warning' 4–5, 79
    meaning of 44–7

principle of assessment practice
    43–4
starting points 126–7
statements of intended outcomes
    150–1
statistical analysis 149–50
students *see* pupils/students;
    teacher–pupil relationship
summative assessment 22–7, 158–9
    change in 162–5
    KOSAP project 111–12, 127, 162–3
    *see also* formative and summative
        assessment; Key Stage
        assessments
supporting learning 16–19, 26–7
    principle of assessment practice
        31–3
sustainability
    concept of 155–7
    conditions associated with 158–62
    of development in assessment
        169–71
    of effective learning environments
        157–8
Sustainable Development Commission
    (SD) 171

teacher advocacy 145
teacher assessment 1–3
    key messages 7–8
    reasons for growing interest in 3–6
teacher beliefs 145
teacher perceptions 144
teacher roles in AfL 64–8
teacher–pupil relationship 22, 27, 35,
    109
Teaching and Learning Research
    Programme (TLRP) 143, 144
teaching process, assessment as part of
    39–40
'test when ready' approach 41
theory *see* principles of assessment
    practice
'top-down' and 'bottom-up' models
    of agency 132–3
    of dissemination 86
    of professional learning 86, 125
tranformation, dissemination as
    91–5
transmission, dissemination as 86–91
transparency and evidence 65, 66

transparent learning environments
109, 119
travelling *vs* embedded policy 91
trial and adjustment model (C) of
professional learning 103, 104,
110, 121, 125
triangulation of evidence 144,
151

understanding 34, 143, 144
unilateralism 137
unintended consequences 151–2
unintentional dissemination 90–1

validity
of evidence 35–7, 82–3
of summative assessment 24, 25
'values and utility' 136, 137
vocational qualifications 63

Wales 56–8, 62–3, 117, 120–1, 164–5,
165–6
Wiliam, D. 23, 38, 117
Black, P. and 21, 23, 38, 73, 75, 104,
105–6, 113–14, 134–5, 166–7
et al. 22, 106, 147–8, 149, 150
Reay, D. and 32, 41, 42